A Guide to

Everyday Economic Statistics

Fifth Edition

Gary E. Clayton
Martin Gerhard Giesbrecht
Both of Northern Kentucky University

McGraw-Hill
Irwin

Boston   Burr Ridge, IL   Dubuque, IA   Madison, WI   New York   San Francisco   St. Louis
Bangkok   Bogotá   Caracas   Lisbon   London   Madrid
Mexico City   Milan   New Delhi   Seoul   Singapore   Sydney   Taipei   Toronto

McGraw-Hill Higher Education

A Division of The McGraw-Hill Companies

A GUIDE TO EVERYDAY ECONOMIC STATISTICS
Gary E. Clayton, Martin Gerhard Giesbrecht

1 2 3 4 5 6 7 8 9 0 DOC/DOC 0 9 8 7 6 5 4 3 2 1 0

ISBN 0-07-243036-2

www.mhhe.com

About the Authors

Gary E. Clayton is Professor of Economics at Northern Kentucky University. He received his Ph.D. in Economics from the University of Utah, has taught and/or lectured on economics and finance at several universities, including the Institute of International Economics and Business at the People's Friendship University of Russia. In addition to his extensive travels, he has authored four books and a number articles in educational, professional, and technical journals. Dr. Clayton has also appeared on a number of radio and television programs and, along with his colleague, Dr. Martin Giesbrecht, has appeared as a guest commentator for "Marketplace," which is broadcast on American Public Radio and originates at the University of Southern California.

Dr. Clayton has a long-standing interest in economic education. He has participated in and/or directed numerous economic education workshops, received an Outstanding Citizen Certificate of Recognition from the state of Arkansas for his work in economic education, and was a national award winner in the college division of the International Paper Company competition which is sponsored by EconomicsAmerica, the National Council on Economic Education. He also writes for the high school market and currently authors the best-selling principles of economics textbook in the country. In March 2000, Dr. Clayton received the prestigious Leavey Award for Excellence in Private Enterprise Education from the Freedoms Foundation in Valley Forge.

Martin Gerhard Giesbrecht is Professor Emeritus of Economics at Northern Kentucky University. He has taught and/or done research at Stanford University, the University of Chicago, Harvard University, Indiana University, National Chengchi University (Taiwan), Rutgers University, and Wilmington College. His doctoral degree (cum laude) was earned at the University of Munich, Germany, which he attended on a Fulbright Grant. Making economics accessible, intellectually enlightening, and even entertaining is the mission of Martin Giesbrecht's professional life. All of his twelve books, including this one, and his many shorter articles, some of which have also appeared in German and Chinese, are dedicated to that end, as are his weekly radio commentaries on WNKU and WMKV.

Because he writes and speaks in a way that people can understand, the Society of Professional Journalism bestowed the Award for Excellence on him in 1993. He has also won awards from the German-American Chamber of Commerce, the National Aeronautics and Space Administration (NASA), the American Society for Engineering Education, the National Science Foundation, The General Electric Foundation, the Ford Foundation, the U.S. Small Business Administration, and the National Endowment for the Humanities, among others. He is especially gratified that the ΦΒΛ (Future Business Leaders) Fraternity voted him their favorite professor on the NKU campus.

Table of Contents

CHAPTER 5: SPENDING, SALES, AND EXPECTATIONS

CHAPTER 6: PRICES, MONEY, AND INTEREST RATES

CHAPTER 7: FINANCIAL MARKETS, INTERNATIONAL TRADE, AND FOREIGN EXCHANGE

Preface

Economic statistics, like so many other lists of numbers, might seem as dry as an old bus schedule. The closer we look at them, however, the more they reveal themselves to be quite fascinating. There are two reasons for this. One, economic statistics hit us where we can feel them: in our breadbaskets, in our wallets, in our standards of living, and in our careers. And, two, they are themselves the products of some of the more extraordinary endeavors of our modern age.

Our everyday economic statistics are important in that they tell us where we have been and show us where we would like to go. Many of these statistics even help us make important personal, family, and business decisions—and so to do without them would be like flying blind or driving cross country without a road map. In short, it's possible, but not advisable. Statistics tell us too much about ourselves and our economy to be left behind unconsidered.

Four years have now passed since the fourth edition of this little guide was published in 1997. It turns out that much has changed, and many of the changes are worthy of note. Specifically, one noteworthy event was the recent "benchmark" overhaul of the National Income and Product Accounts by the U.S. Department of Commerce at the end of 1999. Many of the changes—such as the treatment of computer software purchases as fixed investment expenditures rather than as business expenses—reflect the evolving nature of our increasingly high-tech economy. Another change was to update the base year for constant dollar measures from 1992 to 1996. Other revisions were more technical, methodological, or definitional, but collectively they gave us a much more accurate picture of the overall state of our economy. Furthermore, these revisions are extended back in time, with some affecting series as far back as 1929, to give us a more accurate representation of events that occurred in the past.

Second, accessibility to the data has changed dramatically. Ten years ago, many of the individual series that economists use to keep track of the economy were available on the ECONOMIC BULLETIN BOARD at the U.S. Department of Commerce for a relatively modest cost. In 1995, and as part of a cost-saving measure, many of the most important business cycle series were transferred from the Bureau of Economic Analysis to The Conference Board, a private, non-profit business organization. Since then, however, most federal data-generating agencies have placed their data on the Internet, thereby increasing accessibility and lowering the cost to users.

Third, it is only natural that some statistics take on more importance—and others less so—as time goes on. One such example, the Federal Reserve Bank's *Beige Book*, isn't even statistical in the usual sense of the word. However, the report has become relatively more important as fiscal policy-making in Washington has become increasingly subject to gridlock, thereby making monetary policy—and therefore Fed-watching—all the more important. Finally, yet another interesting series might include the "new jobs created" report that we occasionally hear about, despite the fact that it is only inferred from other data.

That's where this little book comes in, because it is neither a statistics lecture nor an economics textbook. Instead, it is a handy little guide that can be consulted for clarification whenever any of the statistical series dealt with herein are encountered. It examines how the series are constructed and how we may use them effectively. Above all, it tries to put things in context, so the reader can see how an individual statistic relates to the larger picture. Because of this, you won't have to read the book consecutively from beginning to end, although that is OK too.

In these millennial times, many economies and the people living in them are doing better and have better prospects for the future than they have ever had. Countries around the world that were once mired in communism's dogmas or caught in the grip of poverty and underdevelopment are climbing out of these entrapments. We in America seem to have reached an entirely new level of economic performance that is the envy of the rest of the world. Most of the economic news was good during this period as the stock market posted record gains, the unemployment rate reached record lows, the rate of inflation was agreeably low, and productivity surged to new heights. More importantly, in March 2000 the economy set the all-time record for continuous real GDP growth, besting the previous 106 months of continuous expansion during the 1960s. There were some problem areas, of course, as the trade balance and consumer debt levels reached record highs, but all in all, the last four years have been good to us.

At times like this, it might seem less urgent to keep an eye on economic statistics. After all, we may put off watching our diets or keeping tabs on our blood pressures when we are in robust health. But, as more than a few of us have learned, this is precisely the time when concern about our personal well-being is critical. And the same goes for our economic well-being.

That is what this book is all about. Use it well, and use it often.

Gary E. Clayton
Martin Gerhard Giesbrecht

Chapter 1

INTRODUCTION

How the Statistics in This Book Were Chosen

We need economic statistics to know how we are doing, and we need to know how we are doing in order to figure out how to get where we want to go. Decision making requires knowledge, and knowledge is the only logical basis of action. That is why we need economic statistics.

There are literally millions of statistical series! At the personal level, each of us could probably generate a dozen series from our grocery receipts, odometer readings, telephone bills, and electricity bills. Every business, town, city, county, and industry could do and often does the same in its own field of operation.

Even the broad-based measures of economic statistics, those that deal with whole states, regions, and nations, number into the thousands. A glance at any statistical yearbook or almanac or at the annual *Statistical Abstract of the United States*[1] will make this point.

Yet, only a handful of economic statistical series are dealt with in this book. Why?

First and most obvious, there is such a thing as too much information. It can prevent us from seeing the forest for all the trees.

Second, many statistical series, like one detailing our own personal electric consumption, are not interesting to everyone.

---

[1] Available from the Superintendent of Documents, U.S. Government Printing Office, Washington, D.C. 20402. The entire *Statistical Abstract* is also available on the web and can be accessed through the "U.S. Government Publications" section of the http://www.EconSources.com web site.

Third, many statistical series are compiled and published too late to be of much more than historical interest.

Finally, many statistical series are not reported regularly in the press and broadcast media. The small number of series dealt with in this book are those with extremely high profiles. Some, like the Dow Jones Industrial Average, are reported daily—on television, radio, and in national and local newspapers. Others, like the prime rate, are mentioned less frequently, but still receive prominent attention

If we want to know how we are doing or where we are headed, even a handful of series are usually more than enough. They include most of the major economic indicators that are important all of the time. Gross domestic product (GDP), the consumer price index, and the unemployment rate would certainly be in the top half-dozen of anyone's list of key economic statistics. Many others are important most of the time, and the rest are important at least some of the time.

We may not have selected everyone's favorite statistical series—and for that we apologize—but we are driven by a positive philosophy of wanting to describe "what is" rather than a normative one of "what should be." Some statistics are neglected when they should not be, while others are widely reported when there is less reason to do so. However, the objective here is to provide a guide to those series that *do* receive attention rather than to the ones that *should*.

A Frame of Reference

The main measure of overall economic and business activity is gross domestic product, whose fluctuations are the most important gauge of good times or bad times that we have. In this context, as in virtually all others, GDP is to be understood as a final, bottom-line accounting measure, an economic result, rather than as an indicator of things to come.

Many of the statistics reviewed in this book measure either the whole or parts of GDP. Other statistics, the index of leading indicators preeminent among them, serve better as signals of things to come. There are also the more specialized series, such as new housing starts and Standard & Poor's 500 (S&P 500), that serve both as general indicators of future economic activity and as first-order indicators for their own industries. Finally, we have other series such as domestic auto sales that provide important information for their own industries, but have little value as indicators of future economic activity.

As we peruse the formal world of economic statistics, bear in mind that they cannot be evaluated in a vacuum. Statistical series need a background, or a frame of reference, so that they can be put in proper perspective. This the book attempts to do. Sometimes the frame of reference is discussed in terms of the historical development and evolution of the series. Or, the perspective may take the form of a detailed discussion of the way the statistic is measured and compiled. The frame of reference may also be the way the particular indicator or statistic relates to other developments in the economy. In the end, our goal is to provide a perspective that allows for proper interpretation and application of the particular series.

Of particular interest are the three types of indicators—leading lagging, and coincident—shown in Figure 1-1. The name given to each refers to the way the series moves in relation to changes in overall economic activity. For example, the series marked "leading indicator" turns down before the economy enters a recession (the shaded area in the figure) and turns up before the expansion begins.

The "lagging indicator" series behaves just the opposite—it turns down after the economy enters a recession, and up sometime after the recovery is underway. A coincident indicator neither leads nor lags. Instead, its timing is such that it turns down when the economy turns down, and up when the economy turns up.

The three codes in the oval key for each indicator show how the changes in the individual series compare to changes in the overall economy. The coding, also shown in Figure 1-2, is the same as that formerly used by the Bureau of Economic Analysis (BEA) in the Department of Commerce to classify the economic indicators when they were reported in the monthly *Survey of Current Business*.[2]

---

[2] These codes are the closest things we have to being "official" classifications of time series behavior. Unfortunately, they have not been published for some time, so there is no authority on leading, lagging, coincident classification. Instead, we will show the codes where they appear to be relevant, and then encourage the reader to make his or her own judgment as to whether the classification is appropriate.

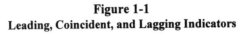

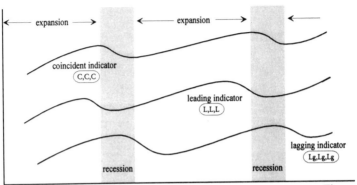

Figure 1-1
Leading, Coincident, and Lagging Indicators

Economic Series

expansion   expansion

coincident indicator
C,C,C

leading indicator
L,L,L

lagging indicator
Lg,Lg,Lg

recession   recession

Time

Economists use the convention of shading recessionary periods to distinguish
them from periods of expansion. Economic series are classified as leading,
coincident, or lagging indicators depending on how their turning points compare
to changes in the overall economy.

Sometimes a series leads both peaks and troughs in the
economy to make it an overall leading indicator. At other times,
it may lead peaks and lag troughs to earn an overall rating of
"unclassified." Other series play no role as indicators of overall
economic activity, and so no classifications are shown.

Whenever possible, the economic series examined in this book
are plotted against the historical background of recessions and
expansions. As will be seen, many series behave like those in Figure
1-1, although the timing of the turning points will vary considerably.
Others will appear to have little, if any, relationship to changes in the
overall economy. Even so, we feel that the presentation is important if
you are to make your own judgments about the behavior of the series.

We have also listed convenient sources for data at the end of
every section. Sometimes the source is in the form of easily
accessible publications, sometimes it is in the form of a web address,

---

Figure 1-2
Leading, Coincident, and Lagging Indicator Codes

(L,Lg,U)   The series leads the peaks in the economy; it turns down *before* the economy turns down (L = leads).
The series lags the economic recovery; it turns up *after* the economy turns up (Lg = lags).
Overall, the series is unclassified; it is neither a leading nor a lagging indicator on a consistent basis (U = unclassified).

(Lg,C,Lg)   The series turns down *after* the economy peaks (Lg = lags).
The series recovers *just as* the economy recovers (C = coincident).
Overall, the series lags (Lg = lags) as an economic indicator.

(C,L,L)   The series turns down *just as* the economy turns down (C = coincident).
The series turns up *before* the economy turns up (L = leads).
Overall, the series is classified as a leading indicator (L = leads) even though the timing of the series is coincident for peaks.

The first code in the oval stands for the timing of the series with respect to peaks in the economy, or when the expansion ends and the recession begins. The second stands for the timing of the series with respect to troughs in the economy, or when the recession ends and the recovery begins. The last code indicates the overall classification of the indicator.

---

and at other times it is in the form of a telephone hotline. In addition, updates to these series, along with many related background articles, can be found in the *Everyday Economic Statistics* section of the http://www.EconSources.com web site.

The Many Faces of Economic Statistics

The task of interpreting economic statistics might seem to be a simple one: just take the numbers and describe how they changed from one period to the next. Unfortunately, it's not always that easy because most statistical series can be reported in a number of ways.

To illustrate, consider a hypothetical report stating that total sales increased by 5 percent from $800 billion to $840 billion over a recent 12-month period. If the report is in terms of current prices, and many initial reports are released this way, then it stands to reason that some of the $40 billion increase is due to inflation.

To compensate for inflation, sales can be measured in terms of "real," "constant," or "chain-linked" dollars using prices that prevailed in an earlier year.[3] If 1996 is used as the base year, and assuming that prices are approximately 10 percent higher now than they were in that base year, the same report could be worded like this: "In terms of chained (1996) prices, total sales increased from $720 billion to $738 billion for the most recent year." This time the increase of $18 billion is only a 2.5 percent gain, so half of the increase current dollar increase was due to inflation, the other half was real growth.

Most series that are susceptible to the distortions of inflation are reported in both current (nominal) and real (constant or chained) dollar amounts, with 1996 being the most recent base year adopted by the U.S. Department of Commerce. Both kinds of information are valuable—if used correctly—although the availability of both means that sales statistics can be reported in a number of different ways:

- the final *current* or *nominal* dollar value of total sales ($840 billion)

- the change in the *current* or *nominal* dollar value of total sales ($40 billion)

- the final *chained*, or *real* dollar value, of total sales ($738 billion)

- the change in *chained*, or *real* dollar value, total sales ($18 billion)

- the percentage change in the *current* or *nominal* dollar sales (5.0 percent, or $40 billion/$800 billion)

- the percentage change in *constant, chain-weighted* or *real dollar sales* (2.5 percent, or $18 billion/$720 billion)

We have the same type of problem when numbers are converted to an index, such as the consumer price index, the producer price index, or any other index. For example, suppose that the index under consideration has a base year of 1977 = 100 and currently stands at

---

3 In January of 1996, the U.S. Department of Commerce switched from a system of base-year fixed prices to a system using chain-weighted geometric averages with 1992 as the reference year. In 1999, the base year was updated to 1996. This technique is described more fully in the Appendix on page 141.

145. If the index goes to 146 in the next month, there is an increase of 1 over the base period activity, or a 0.69 percent increase in the index over the previous month (1/145 = 0.0069). If the index were to grow at the same rate for each of the next 11 months, the annualized rate would be 8.6 percent. [4]

Using the numbers in the paragraph above, we can see that the change in any index can be reported in several different ways:

- the *absolute level* of the index (145)
- the *absolute change* in the level or the index from period to period (1)
- the *relative percentage change* from the previous period (0.69 percent)
- an *annualized projection* of the current period percentage change (8.6 percent)

In general, the relative percentage change is the most useful, with the annualized version coming in next. However, the reader should be advised that even these lists are not exclusive. For example, sometimes the change in the level of the index is compared to a period 12 months earlier. If the new level of 146 is 10 points higher than it was 12 months ago, then we could also say that the annual increase was closer to 7.35 percent.

Abusing Economic Statistics

The governments of the modern, industrialized nations of the free world—the United States among the best of them—enjoy a remarkable reputation for producing honest statistics. Surprisingly (since they bear less responsibility to the citizenry), so do many nongovernmental agencies in these countries that produce statistical series, some of which are included in this book. In some nations however, statistics are exaggerated, underreported, or simply faked for

---

[4] The series is compounding monthly, and so the correct computation is to use the following formula:

$$\text{Annualized growth} = (1 + \text{monthly percentage change})^{12} - 1$$
$$= (1 + 0.0069)^{12} - 1 = 0.086$$

Because of compounding, you cannot multiply the monthly percentage change of 0.0069 by 12 to get an annualized rate, although this mistake is often made!

political or ideological reasons. When this happens, the usefulness of the statistics is radically reduced. Whether they know it or not, it is also a tragic loss to those nations that support this type of activity.

In the United States, our statistics tend to be brutally honest. Agencies that report their statistics normally publish release schedules months in advance of the actual release, and the methodology used to compile the series is remarkable open. As a result, there is not even the slightest hint that the release of new statistical figures is delayed in order to prevent some political or commercial embarrassment.

Perhaps the most common abuse of economic statistics is to apply them to situations for which they were never intended. For example, some series with little, if any, relationship to movements of the overall economy are often treated as if they are significant predictors of future changes in GDP. Personal income in current dollars, discussed in detail in Chapter 4, is one such example. The historical record shows that personal income almost always goes up, even when the economy is in recession.[5] Even so, increases in personal income are dutifully reported and widely heralded by the press each time they are released.

Other series are treated as indicators of future economic activity when, in fact, they are actually coincident or lagging indicators. Interest rates can be cited in this context, especially the prime rate which consistently lags changes in real GDP. Changing interest rates certainly affect selected sectors of the economy, especially housing, automobiles, and to some extent stock prices, but changing interest rates are of little use in predicting future changes in the overall economy.

Yet a third abuse is to focus on nominal dollar values when the real, or inflation-adjusted, figures give a better picture of the underlying changes. Unfortunately, the various government agencies contribute to this problem because the nominal dollar data and the price deflators needed to adjust the data are not available at the same time. When the U.S. Department of Commerce releases its *Advance*

---

[5] The most recent recession in the U.S. economy began in July 1990. During the nine recessionary months that followed, personal income in current dollars increased seven times and declined only twice! In terms of real (chain-weighted) dollars, there were three monthly decreases and six increases.

Monthly Retail Sales report during the second week of every month, the data are adjusted for seasonal, holiday, and trading day differences, but not for inflation. By the time inflation-adjusted figures are available, the initial change in retail sales has already been reported and the new figures are of little interest to the media.

Finally, we should note that the media sometimes report on new economic figures without giving us enough information to evaluate the significance of the numbers. It is not at all unusual to hear that a particular index has gone up, say, 4 points, without any mention of the overall level of the index. Four points on a basis of 40 is one thing, but 4 points on an index with a value of 400 may be quite another.

Using Economic Statistics

Some decision making may require an understanding of other economic conditions, perhaps those that occur at a regional or industry level. Even if the data you need are not described in these chapters (most of the statistics in this book pertain to the national economy), you should be able to use the methods described here to make your own decisions or even build your own set of economic indicators.

If you do, remember that every statistical series has its own distinct personality. If you want to use a series, study it carefully and try to see how it relates to your own situation. For example, are series measured in real, rather than nominal, dollars better for your application? Also, you might examine the series to see if changes in the series are more important than the absolute level of the series. And, what about the timing of the series? If it lags, then it may not be of much help. If it leads, then you may have to spend more time trying to anticipate its movements. If you need regional or industry-specific data, don't forget to look for other sources of data generated by state departments of economic development, chambers of commerce, economic development districts, local universities, and industry and trade publications.

One practical way of organizing economic statistics for your own use is to build your own historical data base of the statistical series that are especially important to you. You can do this with an appropriate spreadsheet program on your personal computer and then graph or otherwise present the results. Yearly entries are probably sufficient for the bygone years; quarterly and monthly data for more recent times will keep you more up-to-date.

To monitor overall economic conditions, you may want to keep tabs on GDP, the consumer price index, the unemployment rate, and several other series, such as the index of leading indicators. To zero in on your own individual area of concern, focus on those series that affect this area more directly. For example, you would examine consumer spending and retail sales if your concern is retail marketing, or the Dow Jones Industrial Average and Standard & Poor's 500 if you're more concerned with the stock market.

As your sophistication grows, this accumulation of statistical data will not only reveal the current state of affairs to you, but you will begin to be able to discern the development of trends. Being able to do this on your own this way, rather than relying on the news media that everybody reads, hears, and watches, gives you that decisive competitive edge that is so important in today's business world. It's mighty useful in your personal affairs too.

Finally, be creative. If the statistics enable you to perceive your economic reality, your economic reality may also enable you to anticipate the statistics. This can be very useful. For example, if your decision is to refinance a mortgage, and if you are waiting for the lowest possible rates, it helps to know that interest rates usually go down during a recession and continue to go down well into the subsequent recovery. So, if the economy appears to be just entering a recession, it might be wise to postpone the refinancing for another six months or a year. Or, if the expansion is well underway, you may want to refinance immediately since interest rates have a history of increasing late in the recovery. In either case, knowledge of how a series relates to the overall economy can be helpful when it comes to forecasting changes in the series.

Finally, bear in mind that—until you become more familiar with the statistics in this book—you don't even have to be an expert to know if the economy is in a recession or an expansion. Just stay tuned to the news, and the media will keep you abreast of developments. Of course the media may miss the beginning or ending of a recession by a few months—and be especially suspect of politicians who make proclamations about the state of the economy during an election year. For the most part, however, those who report on national economic developments in the media usually do a reasonably good job of keeping us posted regarding the state of the economy.

And Beware of Forecasts!

With all of this said, we should also point out that none of this is a formal theory nor a method for making forecasts. Much longer books than this have dealt unsuccessfully with that subject. But we do encounter many large and small forecasts in our daily lives, and these contain fertile opportunities for making statistical trouble. Be forewarned! Here are some things to look out for:

Point Forecasts These are the most common, but they are often wrong because outcomes are unlikely to reach the predicted point precisely. For example, if we predict that the GDP next year will be $10 trillion, we have an almost 100 percent chance of being wrong because next year's GDP might turn up to $10 trillion and 1 cent or any other such number.

Interval Forecasts It is better to say that next year's GDP will be $10 trillion, give or take $50 billion. That means the forecast will turn out to be correct if next year's GDP falls between $9.95 and $10.05 trillion.

Probability Forecasts It is even better to say that next year's GDP has an 85 percent probability of being between $7.95 trillion and $8.05 trillion. This way the confidence with which the forecast is made can be expressed. The higher the probability, the more believable the forecast should be, assuming that the forecaster is reputable.

Unconditional Forecasts All of the above examples fall into this category because, unlike the conditional forecast below, they are not premised on some second event taking place.

Conditional Forecasts "There is an 85 percent probability that next year's GDP will be between $9.95 trillion and $10.05 trillion if the Federal Reserve System does not raise the discount rate" is a conditional forecast because all bets are off if the Fed does raise the discount rate. This gives the forecaster an "out" if the forecast turns out to be wrong, but it also makes the forecast a bit less useful to the user.

Event Forecasts All the above examples fall into this category, because they deal with a single event, a single outcome.

Time Series Forecasts A series of forecasts that march into the future by convenient time steps–weeks, months, quarters, or years–are much more complicated than a single-event forecast. For example, forecasting that "the GDP next year will grow at an annual rate of 4 percent during the first 6 months and then slow to 3 percent in the last half of the year" is actually making at least two forecasts. Since the second one is probably dependent on the accurate outcome of the first, this kind of forecasting can be tricky. Rate-of-change-over-time forecasts are especially susceptible to this complication.

Extrapolation Forecasts Extrapolation from a monthly figure is often taken as a kind of time series forecast. For example, a monthly increase of 0.69 percent converts to an annual rate of 8.6 percent, if the next 11 months are identical to the most recent one.

Weighted Moving Average Forecasts If a particular series is subject to considerable fluctuation, a moving average with specific weights assigned to earlier periods can be used to smooth the data.[6] When this technique is adapted to forecasting, it is easier to predict the next number in the average since a portion of the data used to construct it is already in hand. And, with our attention focused on the moving average, the forecaster can even be excused if the next new observation "deviates" from the mean.

Many of the forecasts that we encounter in the daily news have considerable value. Many others, however, have little or no value since we are not clear as to what kind of forecast they are or how they have been constructed. They often use hedging or waffling language that, when carefully read or listened to, pulls the rug of credibility out from underneath them. Even worse, many are based on other statistics that may not be well-suited for the forecast being made.

A Final Word

Throughout, this book tries to be ideologically and theoretically neutral or at least conventional. Notice that the economic indicators described in the following chapters are grouped primarily by economic function rather than by alphabet or other method. This is to recognize implicitly that, while no formal theoretical or ideological

---

[6] Statistics on changes in manufacturing and trade inventories are smoothed using a four-term weighted average with weights of 1, 2, 2, 1. To illustrate, changes of $-47.2, $68.2, $64.1, and $40.3 billion (the numbers for June, July, August, and September of 1990) yield a moving average of $42.95 billion for the month of September.

statement is intended, our economy is nevertheless a functioning system made up of identifiable parts that somehow work together.

And remember: we should never become so blinded by the apparent numerical precision and by the "scientific," "theoretical," or "official" nature of these economic indicators that we ignore our own sensitivity to economic and business conditions. Our own observations may be rather parochial, but they are immediate and undisputably real. Keeping an eye on the amount of construction activity in the neighborhood where we live, the intensity of traffic on our streets, how hard or easy it is to find a place to park, what and how much people are buying in the stores where we shop, the number of layoffs or job promotions among our friends and acquaintances, the level of maintenance and upkeep in our surrounding buildings and grounds, and even the changes in the frequency of marriages and new babies in our communities can all be very revealing. We ourselves are, after all, living daily in the very economy we are trying to understand.

This economic awareness, this "feel" for business conditions should be extended to our interpretations of the statistical series as well. We can examine the way statistical series are constructed, and we can look at the historical record to see how they behave. But in the end, it comes down to developing a feel for what they really tell us.

Chapter 2

TOTAL OUTPUT, PRODUCTION, AND GROWTH

Gross Domestic Product

The most comprehensive measure of production is **gross domestic product (GDP)**–the market value of all final goods, services, and structures produced in one year by labor and property located in the United States, regardless of who owns the resources.[1] GDP is the summary statistic that comes from our national income and product accounts (NIPA) compiled by the Bureau of Economic Analysis in the U.S. Department of Commerce. The NIPA and its components are the most exhaustive statistical collection efforts ever undertaken.

The need to know more about the economy became apparent during the Great Depression of the 1930s when it was discovered that our information about overall economic performance was limited at best. Pioneering work on GDP and the national income accounts was done by Dr. Simon Kuznets in the early 1930's who later received the Nobel Prize for his efforts. The measure has been continually refined and improved since then, and in December of 1999, the U.S. Department of Commerce announced that the development of GDP and NIPA was "its achievement of the century."[2]

---

[1] In 1991, GDP replaced *gross national product (GNP)*, a measure of the total income produced in one year with labor and property supplied by U.S. residents, regardless of where the resources are located. The conversion to GDP made the measurement of total output consistent with the system of accounts used by the World Bank and most other industrial nations.

[2] "GDP: One of the Great Inventions of the 20th Century," *Survey of Current Business*, January 2000.

How Is GDP Measured?

Although GDP is a comprehensive measure, it is not practical to record every final good, service, or structure produced in the course of one year. Instead, sampling techniques are used and projections are made from the samples.

It helps to think of the analysis as being divided into two parts. The first involves a count of the number of final goods, services, and structures produced. The second involves assigning a dollar value to the output. The two are multiplied together and then summed to get a measure of total output. If current prices are used, then the measure is simply *GDP*, or *GDP in current prices*. If we want to adjust for the distortions of inflation, base year prices are selected (1996 is currently used), and then adjusted for relative price changes, to give us *real GDP*, or *GDP in constant (1996) dollars*.

Table 2-1 illustrates both types of computations for the U.S. economy in the first quarter of 2000 (sometimes denoted 2000-I). Suppose that the items in the first column represent actual production in that year. If output is valued at prices that existed at the time, the total value of production—or GDP in current dollars—is taking place at an annual rate of $9,697.2 billion. In the bottom part of the table, the same output is computed using 1996 chain weighted prices to give us a value of $9,156.6 billion.[3]

---

[3] In the first quarter of 1996, the U.S. Department of Commerce switched from a system of 1987 fixed-weight prices to a "chain-linked" set of prices. The difficulty with the former measure was that some prices, such as computer prices which declined an average of 13 percent annually since 1987, changed relative to other prices over time.

To illustrate, suppose that X number of computers were made in 1987 at an average price of Y, resulting in a contribution to GDP of XY (X times Y). If we jump ahead ten years and let X' represent the number of computers made in 1997 (hundreds, if not thousands, of times as many as in 1987), and if they are valued at the average computer price, Y, that prevailed in 1987, then the dollar value computer component (X'Y) of GDP would be overstated. An alternative approach would be to adjust the average cost of computers downward by an average of 13 percent annually to a point where the average 1997 price was Y', so that the GDP contribution in that year amounts to X'Y'.

The phrase "chain-weighted" or "chain-linked" refers to the manner in which percentage increases are computed from one year to the next. For example, under the old method, prices from an earlier year were used to value output that was produced in a later period. Under the new method, the weighting is done with prices from both years using a geometric mean that economists call the "Fisher Ideal." A brief numerical example of this computation also appears in the Appendix on page 141.

Table 2-1

Computation of GDP in Current and Constant (Chained) Dollars

(A) GDP in Current Prices:

Annual Domestic Output		Quantity in millions	Current Prices	Value in billions of $
Goods:	Automobiles	7	$19,500	$136.5
	Chairs	5	80	4.0
	..... Other	–	–	–
Services:	Legal	8	550	4.4
	Child care/wk	3	100	0.3
	..... Other	–	–	–
Structures:	Residential	1.4	140,000	196.0
	Commercial	1	340,000	340.0
	..... Other	–	–	–
	GDP in current dollars			*$9,697.2*

(B) Current GDP (chained 1996 dollars):

Annual Domestic Output		Quantity in millions	1996 Dollars	Value in billions of $
Goods:	Automobiles	7	$16,219	$113.5
	Chairs	5	100	0.1
	..... Other	–	–	–
Services:	Legal	8	412	3.3
	Child care/wk	3	60	0.2
	..... Other	–	–	–
Structures:	Residential	1.4	114,740	160.6
	Commercial	1	69,469	269.5
	..... Other	–	–	–
	GDP in constant dollars			*$9,156.6*

Note: $9,697.2 and $9,156.6 are 2000-I advanced estimates, and hence subject to change.

The advantage of using chain-linked prices is that it enables us to compare the annual rate of total output in the first quarter of 2001 to the third quarter of 1995, or to any other year and quarter for that matter. So if real or constant GDP changes by 1 or 2 percent, the difference must be due to changes in the number of goods, services, and/or structures produced after compensating for changes in price levels. The increase *cannot* be due to distortions caused by inflation.[4]

---

[4] Whenever a series is expressed in "real" terms, only the *percentage change* is relevant, not the dollar or index value of the series. When we focus on percentage changes, the choice of the base year is not important.

Does GDP Overlook Anything?

You bet! For example, GDP tells us nothing about the mix, or *composition* of output. A bigger GDP only tells us that the dollar value of total output increased. We don't know if the increase was due to the production of new roads, homes, schools, and libraries—or to the increased production of nerve gas, B-1 bombers, and toxic waste landfills. Also, GDP doesn't tell us anything about the *quality of life*. For example, you might feel that the quality of life is enhanced every time a city park or museum is built instead of a nuclear reactor.

Perhaps the biggest limitation is that GDP excludes nonmarket activities, such as the services performed by homemakers and the services people perform for themselves. For example, GDP will go down if a homeowner marries his or her housekeeper and does not hire a replacement. Likewise, GDP will go up if you hire someone to mow your own yard, but it will not go up if you do it yourself.

Other activities—prostitution, gambling, and drug running—are mostly illegal and are simply not reported to the IRS, Department of Commerce, or anyone else. These activities are part of the underground economy and are not directly included in GDP, although estimates are made for their inclusion.[5]

GDP Estimates and Revisions

Even though GDP does not try to include everything, measurement is still a formidable task. To keep the numbers as current as possible, GDP estimates are made quarterly, and additional revisions are made as new data become available. The Bureau of Economic Analysis (BEA) in the U.S. Department of Commerce releases three estimates according to the following schedule:[6]

Advance – released near the end of the *first* month after the end of the quarter.

Preliminary – released near the end of *second* month after end of the quarter.

Final – released near the end of the *third* month after the end of the quarter.

---

5 In December 1985, GNP statistics extending back to 1929 were revised upward to account for the unreported underground economy activity. As a result of the revision, GNP in 1984 was increased by $119.9 billion and these revisions are now part of GDP. Even so, some private sector economists think that these revisions were not large enough.

6 The full schedule of BEA news releases which contains upcoming release dates and times can be found on their web site at http://www.bea.doc.gov.

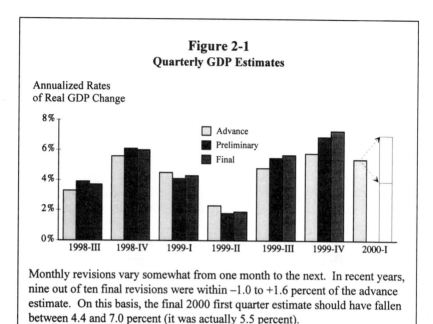

Figure 2-1
Quarterly GDP Estimates

Annualized Rates
of Real GDP Change

Monthly revisions vary somewhat from one month to the next. In recent years, nine out of ten final revisions were within −1.0 to +1.6 percent of the advance estimate. On this basis, the final 2000 first quarter estimate should have fallen between 4.4 and 7.0 percent (it was actually 5.5 percent).

Figure 2-1 above shows the three GDP estimates from the third quarter of 1998 through the first quarter of 2000. These quarterly estimates are reported on an annualized basis—which means that this is the rate at which the economy would grow for a twelve-month period if the growth in the other three quarters was the same as the current one. Since this is seldom the case, the final figures for the year will be slightly different. As a result, many observers tend to focus on the direction of change rather than on the absolute level.

Because of the revisions and delays in getting the estimates, we really don't know how the economy fared during a particular quarter until nearly three months later—and even these estimates are reviewed annually every July for the most recent calendar year and the two preceding years. For example, in July 2000, the final GDP figures for 1997, 1998, and 1999 will all be revised.

A more comprehensive revision, also known as a benchmark revision, is carried out at approximately 5-year intervals, with the last being completed at the end of 1999. These changes can be extensive and mean that we never have the luxury of just adding the latest numbers to an existing time series such as that shown in Figure 2-2 on page 21. Instead, we always have to obtain the most recent revisions regardless of whether our interest is in long-term trends or simply changes from one month to the next.

To illustrate, the biggest change in the most recent benchmark revision was to treat software purchases as capital investment, rather than to treat it as a business expense. This revision caused an increase in the level of GDP that extended back to 1959.[7] A variety of lesser methodological and statistical changes were also implemented to take advantage of the myriad of other statistics currently available, thereby improving the quality of GDP estimates. To make GDP changes easier to understand, some tables were dropped and others added—especially two designed to show the percentage contributions to GDP made by the individual entries such as equipment and software. Finally, a lesser change revised the base year from 1992 to 1996.

How Reliable Are the Monthly Estimates?

The monthly revisions provide surprisingly reliable results. A recent study by the BEA found that each of the three estimates—advance, preliminary, and final—provide reliable indications of the *direction* of real GDP change 98 percent of the time. In addition, they provide reliable indications of the *rate* of change (accelerating or decelerating rates of growth) about 75 percent of the time.[8]

In addition, the size of the monthly revision is usually not very large when compared to the advance estimate, the first estimate made for the quarter. In fact, two-thirds of the time, the final revision falls within –0.5 percent to +1.0 percent of the advance estimate. When all of these factors are taken into account, it turns out that the advance estimate for any one quarter—despite the fact that it is revised almost continually—is a fairly reliable statistic.

---

[7] A detailed summary of this and other changes can be found in "A Preview of the 1999 Comprehensive Revision of the National Income and Product Accounts—Definitional and Classificational Changes," by Moulton, Parker, and Seskin, *Survey of Current Business*, August 1999. This article can also be downloaded in PDF format from the EconSources.com web site.

[8] Grimm, Bruce T., and Parker, Robert P., "Reliability of the Quarterly and Annual Estimates of GDP and Gross Domestic Income," *Survey of Current Business*, December 1998. The survey covered a 60-quarter period beginning in 1983 and ending in 1997.

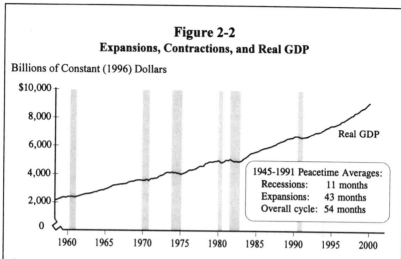

Figure 2-2
Expansions, Contractions, and Real GDP

Billions of Constant (1996) Dollars

1945-1991 Peacetime Averages:
Recessions: 11 months
Expansions: 43 months
Overall cycle: 54 months

Real GDP

Some economists prefer to talk in terms of business *cycles*, which implies systematic changes in real GDP marked by alternating periods of expansion and contraction. Others prefer to talk of *fluctuations*, which implies alternating, but not systematic, periods of expansion and contraction. The shaded areas in the figure represent recession years. The expansion since March of 1991 is the longest in United States history.

When Is the Economy in a Recession?

A recession occurs whenever real GDP declines for two consecutive quarters. However, the exact date a recession begins and ends is not determined by the Bureau of Economic Analysis, the Department of Commerce, or any other government agency. Instead, the turning points are determined by the National Bureau of Economic Research (NBER), a prestigious private research institute with a long and distinguished record of research into the cause and measurement of business cycles.[9]

---

[9] The members of the NBER business cycle dating committee that determined the dates for the 1990-91 recession were: Robert E. Hall of the Hoover Institute at Stanford University (chairman of the dating committee), Geoffry Moore of Columbia University, Robert J. Gordon of Northwestern University, Benjamin M. Friedman of Harvard University, Victor Zarnowitz of the University of Chicago, William Branson of Princeton University, and Martin Feldstein of Harvard University (also president of the NBER).

Because recessions have become increasingly infrequent, however, the membership of the business cycle dating committee will be different in the future.

Table 2-2
Business Cycle Expansions and Contractions in the United States

Peak	Trough	Peak	Recession	Expansion	Cycle
			Duration in Months[*]		
October 1860	June 1861	April 1865	8	*46*	*54*
April 1865	December 1867	June 1869	*32*	18	*50*
June 1869	December 1870	October 1873	18	34	52
October 1873	March 1879	March 1882	65	36	101
March 1882	May 1885	March 1887	38	22	60
March 1887	April 1888	July 1890	13	27	40
July 1890	May 1891	January 1893	10	20	30
January 1893	June 1894	December 1895	17	18	35
December 1895	June 1897	June 1899	18	24	42
June 1899	December 1900	September 1902	18	21	39
September 1902	August 1904	May 1907	23	33	56
May 1907	June 1908	January 1910	13	19	32
January 1910	January 1912	January 1913	24	12	36
January 1913	December 1914	August 1918	23	*44*	*67*
August 1918	March 1919	January 1920	*7*	10	*17*
January 1920	July 1921	May 1923	18	22	40
May 1923	July 1924	October 1926	14	27	41
October 1926	November 1927	August 1929	13	21	34
August 1929	March 1933	May 1937	43	50	93
May 1937	June 1938	February 1945	13	*80*	*93*
February 1945	October 1945	November 1948	*8*	37	*45*
November 1948	October 1949	July 1953	11	*45*	*56*
July 1953	May 1954	August 1957	*10*	39	*49*
August 1957	April 1958	April 1960	8	24	32
April 1960	February 1961	December 1969	10	*106*	*116*
December 1969	November 1970	November 1973	*11*	36	*47*
November 1973	March 1975	January 1980	16	58	74
January 1980	July 1980	July 1981	6	12	18
July 1981	November 1982	July 1990	16	92	108
July 1990	March 1991		8	–	–

Averages for peacetime cycles (recession and expansion) only:[*]

	Recession	Expansion	Cycle
1854-1991 (26 cycles)	19	27	48
1854-1919 (14 cycles)	22	24	47
1919-1945 (5 cycles)	20	26	45
1945-1991 (7 cycles)	11	43	54

[*]Cycles are measured from peak-to-peak, a trough-to-trough measurement gives different durations, the underscored figures are wartime periods.
Source: National Bureau of Economic Research and the *Survey of Current Business.*

Because the NBER wants to determine the turning points as accurately as possible, it considers as much data as it can, most of it monthly. As a result, the official turning points listed in Table 2-2 may not always coincide with quarterly changes in real GDP. For example, even though real GDP growth did not become negative until second and third quarters of 1980 (April through September), the NBER business cycle dating committee determined that the recession began in January of that year and ended in July.[10]

In addition, turning point decisions rendered by the NBER are even much slower than quarterly GDP estimates. According to the NBER, the record expansion that began in late 1982 ended in July 1990. However, the July turning point determination was not made until much later in May of 1991 after members of the NBER business cycle dating committee examined historical data on jobs, personal income, industrial production, and retail, manufacturing, and trade sales. Likewise, the official ending date of March 1991 was not announced until December 1992—nearly 21 months later.

How Are Other Statistics Related to GDP?

Good question! In fact, most of the statistics reported in this book are related to GDP in one way or another. Some statistics report on the various components of total output—goods, services, structures—shown in Table 2-1. Other series track subcategories like durable and nondurable goods, and even others are used to track the production of product categories like automobiles and residential housing.

The most popular presentation of GDP is shown in Table 2-3. This format features the consumption of total output by four major sectors—consumer, business, foreign, and government. Some statistics are designed to track these major categories, while other statistics are designed to help predict future changes in the level of GDP or one of its components.

---

[10] Comprehensive revisions of the NIPA accounts extending back to 1929 are bound to change some of the earlier numbers, whereas the NBER dates are not revised. Pre-revision numbers show the decline in real GDP taking place in the *first* two quarters of 1980, not the second and third! For more detail on the revised source data, see Moulton and Seskin, "A Preview of the 1999 Comprehensive Revision of the National Income and Product Accounts, Statistical Changes," *Survey of Current Business*, October 1999.

Table 2-3
The National Income and Product Accounts,
First Quarter 2000 Advance Annual Estimates – Billions of Dollars

	Current	Constant (1996$)	% GDP
Gross domestic product	*$9,697.2*	*$9,156.6*	*100.0*
Personal consumption expenditures	*6,615.2*	*6,225.2*	*68.2*
Durable goods	825.5	898.1	8.5
Nondurable goods	1,963.3	1,842.4	20.2
Services	3,826.5	3,500.6	39.5
Gross private domestic investment	*1,709.9*	*1,724.2*	*17.6*
Fixed investment	1,675.4	1,683.7	17.3
Nonresidential	1,248.6	1,304.6	12.9
Structures	285.4	253.6	2.9
Equipment and software	963.2	1,061.4	9.9
Residential	426.8	382.9	4.4
Change in private inventories	34.4	31.1	0.4
Net exports of goods and services	*-335.0*	*-377.1*	*-3.5*
Exports	1,043.7	1,077.7	10.8
Imports	1,378.7	1,454.8	14.2
Government consumption & gross investment	*1,707.1*	*1,565.2*	*17.6*
Federal	579.2	535.2	6.0
National defense	363.7	339.2	3.8
Nondefense	215.5	195.8	2.2
State and local	1,127.9	1,029.4	11.6

Source: *Survey of Current Business*. The first column shows entries in terms of current dollars, the second column shows "real" or constant dollar entries which are based on chain weighting calculations discussed in Appendix B (also, note that one of the idiosyncrasies of chain weighting is that "real" dollar amounts are sometimes larger than current dollar amounts). The percent of GDP column is based on current dollars; percentages are slightly different for chain weighted dollars. Some totals may not agree because of rounding.

Finally, whenever GDP is produced, income is generated in the form of wages and salaries, interest, rents, and profits. Since the recipients of this income eventually spend it, even more statistics are kept on the income, and/or spending of these groups. Almost every statistic, then, is related to GDP in one way or another.

The New Summary Tables

It is difficult to comprehend a statistic that is measured in trillions of dollars—as is the case with GDP. Because of this, the U.S.

Table 2-4
Summary of Contributions to Percent Change in Real GDP
Percent Change at Annual Rates – First Quarter 2000 Advance Estimates

	1999-II	1999-III	1999-IV	2000-I
Gross domestic product	*1.9*	*5.7*	*7.3*	*5.4*
Personal consumption expenditures	*3.36*	*3.33*	*4.07*	*5.50*
Durable goods	0.71	0.62	1.03	2.00
Nondurable goods	0.64	0.73	1.51	1.37
Services	2.00	1.98	1.53	2.14
Gross private domestic investment	*-0.36*	*2.26*	*1.72*	*1.38*
Fixed investment	1.10	1.16	0.48	2.77
Nonresidential	0.86	1.33	0.39	2.48
Structures	-0.16	-0.11	-0.01	0.37
Equipment and software	1.02	1.44	0.40	2.10
Residential	0.24	-0.17	0.09	0.29
Change in private inventories	-1.46	1.09	1.24	-1.39
Net exports of goods and services	*-1.35*	*-0.73*	*-0.12*	*-1.31*
Exports	0.42	1.19	1.08	-0.01
Imports	-1.77	-1.92	-1.20	-1.30
Government consumption & gross investment	*0.23*	*0.81*	*1.61*	*-0.18*
Federal	0.13	0.26	0.87	-1.03
National defense	-0.10	0.42	0.65	-1.03
Nondefense	0.23	-0.16	0.22	0.00
State and local	0.10	0.55	0.75	0.85

Source: Table S.2, first quarter advance GDP estimates, Bureau of Economic Analysis.

Department of Commerce introduced two new summary tables when it completed the 1999 comprehensive benchmark revision of the national income and product accounts.[11] The first table shows how each component has changed from the preceding period. The second, shown as Table 2-4 above, shows the contribution to the total GDP change made by individual components.

According Table 2-4, real GDP increased at an annual rate of 5.4 percent in the first quarter of 2000. The largest contribution was

---

[11]A simple example illustrates the magnitude of the numbers involved in GDP, and of the logic for focusing on percentage changes rather than absolute amounts: A dollar bill is about 6 inches (15.2 cm) long, so if $9.7 trillion dollar bills (approximately the size of the annual GDP estimated in the first quarter 2000) were laid end to end, they would stretch from the surface of the earth to the sun and back—not once, but a total of *five* round trips.

due to personal consumption expenditures which, along with increases in gross private domestic investment, was large enough to offset declines in net exports of goods and services and government consumption expenditures.

Each of these four main categories is further broken down to show the contribution made by the various subcategories. For example, we can see from the table that nearly half of the annual 5.4 percentage growth rate for the quarter, or 2.1 points, came from the equipment and software category. The production of services was another strong contributor, as was the category of durable goods.

GDP – A Measure of Output Or Welfare?

Occasionally, GDP is criticized on the grounds that it does not adequately measure our welfare, or our overall feeling of well-being. Do increases in GDP mean that we are really better off, one might ask—especially during times of urban sprawl, environmental congestion, increasing divorce rates, and so on?[12] The short answer is that no single series could ever be comprehensive enough to take into account all of the factors that make us happy or unhappy. However, there is some truth to the assertion that GDP is at least a partial measure of welfare.

The reason for this—and one of the fundamental assumptions of economics—is that a market economy is based on *voluntary* transactions. For example, whenever you buy something that was just produced (a transaction reflected in the GDP), you must have felt that the money you gave up was worth less to you than the product you acquired—otherwise you would not have made the transaction. Likewise, the producer felt that the product given up was worth less than the money received—or the producer would not have made the sale. In the end, the exchange took place because both parties felt that they were better off after the transaction than they were before it took place.

We need to remember that GDP was designed as a measure of total output, not as an overall measure of welfare—so those who claim that it fails in this regard really miss the mark. The fact that GDP can

---

12 Cobb, Halstead, and Rowe, "If the GDP is Up, Why is America Down?" *Atlantic Monthly*, October, 1995.

tell us anything about welfare should be considered as a plus, and we should be looking at the glass as if it were half full, rather than half empty.

One of the Great Invention of the 20th Century

Economists, as you can tell by now, are passionate about their work, and they are passionate about their statistics, especially GDP and the national income and product accounts that support it. This endeavor is truly one of the remarkable efforts of our time, and the recognition the U.S. Department of Commerce bestowed on these efforts is well-deserved. GDP truly is "one of the great inventions of the 20th century."

Gross Domestic Product in Brief	
Compiled by:	Bureau of Economic Analysis, U.S. Department of Commerce
Frequency:	Quarterly
Release date:	Advance estimate at the end of the first month following the end of the quarter
Revisions:	Two monthly revisions following the advance estimate, annual revisions in July for 3 years, comprehensive or "benchmark" revisions every 5 years
Published data:	*Economic Indicators*, Council of Economic Advisors *Survey of Current Business*, U.S. Department of Commerce
Internet:	http://www.bea.doc.gov http://www.EconSources.com
Hotline update:	(202)606-5306 for a short recorded message

Index of Industrial Production

The *index of industrial production* is a comprehensive index of industrial activity compiled by the Board of Governors of the Federal Reserve System. Because of the Fed's responsibility for monetary policy, and because of delays in reporting final GDP, the index is designed to give the Fed a quicker reading on the overall health and activity of the manufacturing sector of the economy. The index is compiled monthly and released approximately midmonth of the following month.

The overall index is made up 267 individual series that represent 26 major industries. The data are collected directly from a number of sources, including gas and electric utilities, the Bureau of Mines, the Bureau of the Census, other government agencies, and industry trade associations.[13] After the source data are collected, compiled, and weighted according to the respective industry size, they are expressed as a percentage of 1992 base-year output.

Industrial Production and GDP

If we break the first quarter 2000 advance estimate for GDP down by type of product as in Figure 2-3, we can see that the goods category amounted to 37.8 percent of total output. This is the segment of the economy tracked by the index of industrial production.

Industrial production is usually reported in one of several ways: the first is the *total index*, which is a compilation of all individual indices. The total index is also presented by major market groups— with sub-categories for consumer goods, business equipment, and construction supplies—and by major industry groups to highlight activity in the manufacturing, mining, and utilities industries.

---

13 Oddly enough, the Fed uses some *quarterly* series to compile the *monthly* index of industrial production. Specifically, quarterly data from Dataquest, a private agency, is used to determine real output in the computer industry. The Fed does this by making monthly estimates which are then revised as the quarterly data become available.

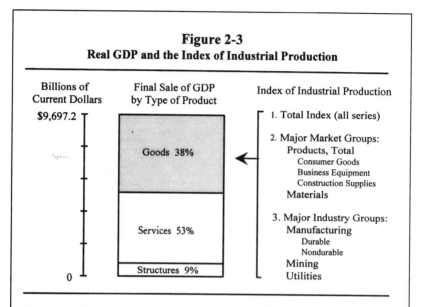

Figure 2-3
Real GDP and the Index of Industrial Production

Billions of Current Dollars	Final Sale of GDP by Type of Product	Index of Industrial Production
$9,697.2	Goods 38%	1. Total Index (all series)
		2. Major Market Groups: Products, Total
		Consumer Goods
		Business Equipment
		Construction Supplies
		Materials
	Services 53%	3. Major Industry Groups: Manufacturing
		Durable
		Nondurable
	Structures 9%	Mining
0		Utilities

The index of industrial production is made up of 267 individual series that track slightly more than one-third of GDP. Breakdowns of the total index are provided for both major market and major industry groups.

Monthly Estimates and Revisions

The initial release of the index of industrial production, like most other economic data, is subject to considerable revision. The process is complicated by the fact that the overall index is made up of so many different series, most of which become available at separate times, and some of which are themselves subject to further revision.

The Fed deals with this problem by substituting its own estimates for missing data if data have not yet been received. To illustrate, electric power usage data are not available when the initial report is issued, so the Fed makes a judgment as to what it thinks the numbers will be. The same is done for other missing data, so slightly more than half of the initial release is based the Fed's own estimates.[14] Then, as better data become available over the next three months, it is used in place of the Fed's own estimates.

---

[14] Gilbert, Morin, and Raddock, "Industrial Production and Capacity Utilization: Recent Developments and the 1999 Revision," *Federal Reserve Bulletin*, March 2000.

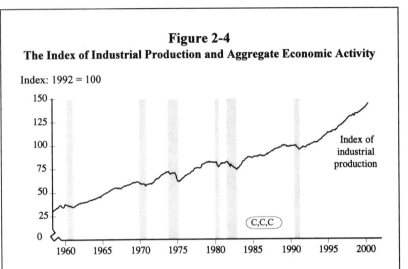

Figure 2-4

The Index of Industrial Production and Aggregate Economic Activity

Index: 1992 = 100

The index of industrial production behaves as a coincident indicator, with changes in production taking place at about the same time as changes in the direction of overall economic activity.

Despite these revisions, the initial release is fairly reliable. In fact, whenever the Fed releases the initial industrial production number for the month, it shows both the previous and the revised estimates for the preceding three months.

What About the Historical Record?

Figure 2-4 shows that the total index of industrial production tends to behave as a coincident indicator, meaning that the peaks and troughs in the series occur at approximately the same time as the economy peaks and troughs. This is to be expected, since overall industrial production represents such a large proportion of total GDP.

When the durable and nondurable goods series are presented separately, as shown in Figure 2-5, it is evident that the durable goods portion of the index is more volatile. This normally occurs because the purchase of durable goods—automobiles, furniture, and appliances that last more than three years under normal use—can usually be postponed if consumers find themselves short of cash.

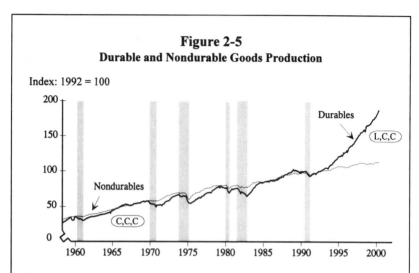

Figure 2-5
Durable and Nondurable Goods Production

Index: 1992 = 100

The durable goods component of the industrial production index is slightly more volatile than nondurables. The durables index also seems to do a slightly better job when it comes to predicting recessions, but they are both coincident overall.

Whenever a series has turning points that coincident with the turning points of overall economic activity, we get a reasonably good reading on the current state of the economy—which is exactly what the Fed wants when it makes its monetary policy decisions.

The Index of Industrial Production in Brief

Indicator status:	Coincident with changes in real GDP
Compiled by:	Federal Reserve System Board of Governors
Frequency:	Monthly
Release date:	Preliminary estimate around the fifteenth of the following month
Revisions:	Preliminary estimate subject to revision in each of the subsequent 3 months, annual revision every fall for the previous 2 years, benchmark revision every 5 years
Published data:	*Economic Indicators*, Council of Economic Advisors *Statistical Release G.17*, Federal Reserve System
Internet:	http://www.bog.frb.fed.us http://www.EconSources.com
Hotline update:	None

Index of Leading Indicators

One of the most interesting, and occasionally controversial, statistical series is the composite *index of leading indicators*, a monthly series designed to tell us where the economy is headed. Essentially, the series is a predictive tool to tell us if, and approximately when, a recession might take place.

The series is released by The Conference Board at the beginning of every month and is calculated from a variety of government series released during the previous month.[15] It is widely followed and often reported in the form of a brief chart such as the one shown in Figure 2-6 below.

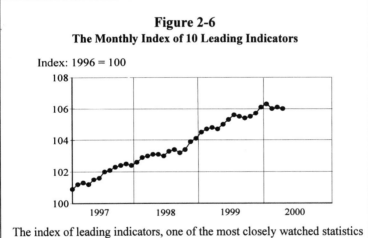

Figure 2-6
The Monthly Index of 10 Leading Indicators

Index: 1996 = 100

The index of leading indicators, one of the most closely watched statistics in the economy today, has provided (on average) a 12-month warning of impending recessions.

---

[15] The series was compiled by the U.S. Department of Commerce for almost 30 years, but was transferred to The Conference Board in December of 1995 as part of a budget-saving measure. The Conference Board is a private, not-for-profit, non-advocacy organization that publishes several other statistical series including help-wanted, consumer confidence, and business confidence indices.

How Do We Interpret the Index?

In general, most observers focus on changes in the direction and duration of the index. For example, if the index declines for three consecutive months, the conventional wisdom is that the index has signaled that a recession is about to begin.

In the same way, three consecutive monthly increases are taken as a sign that the economy will prosper or continue to prosper. The most difficult case to interpret is one where the index goes up for several months and then down for several months—or moves in no particular pattern—as it did in early 2000.

How Was the Index Developed?

Intuitively, the concept of a leading indicator is fairly easy to grasp. We start with the observation that the overall economyis made up of all types of economic activity. Next we ask, could it be that some activities take place or that some events occur in *advance* of changes in the overall economy? If so, perhaps we could focus on these activities and use them to predict howthe entire economy might behave in the near future.

Back in the 1950s, the National Bureau of Economic Research thought this might be happening, and so they compared thousands of statistical series to changes in real GNP (GDP is now used instead). One set of data examined was an index of stock prices, which, as it turned out, usually declined sharply just before a recession got underway.

Theoretically, the linkage between stock prices and overall spending makes sense. For example, if people feel poorerbecause of their losses in the market, they might decide to cut back on spending. If enough people feel poorer, their collective decision to spend less may actually affect economic growth.

By itself, however, a measure of stock price performance could not be used as the sole indicator of future economic activity because stock prices sometimes went down while the economy kept going up. Using the approach that there is safety in numbers, why not look for some other statistical series to combine with stock prices?

It turned out that building permits for private housing also behaved somewhat like stock prices—with the total number of permits issued tending to decrease several months before the economy turned down. Again, this seems to make sense because a decline in building permits may well mean that a substantial amount of economic activity will either be delayed or not take place at all.

Eventually, the list was narrowed down to a handful and then combined to form a composite index. The resulting series usually changed direction some months *before* the economy did, hence the term "leading indicator." The index offered considerable promise, and so the Department of Commerce took over the task of collecting and publishing the data. Eventually, responsibility for compiling the series was transferred to The Conference Board, making it the first-ever privatization of an official U.S. government statistical series.

The list of component series in the index is presented in Table 2-5. The Department of Commerce revised the list in 1989, and it was

Table 2-5
The Index of 10 Leading Indicators, Individual Components

1. Average weekly hours of production workers in manufacturing
2. Average weekly initial claims for state unemployment insurance
3. Manufacturers' new orders for consumer goods/materials
4. Vendor performance–slower deliveries diffusion index
5. Manufacturers' new orders, nondefense capital goods
6. New private housing authorized by local building permits
7. Stock prices, 500 common stocks
8. Money supply, M2
9. Interest rate spread, 10-year Treasury bonds less federal funds rate
10. Index of consumer expectations (University of Michigan series)

Source: The Conference Board, May 2000

revised again by The Conference Board in December of 1996. The last revision dropped two series in favor of the yield curve which is a measure of the spread between long-term and short-term interest rates.[16] This revision also made it an index of 10 (rather than 11) indicators, but the major concern is whether the performance of the index can be improved, not the number of individual components.

---

16 The series that were dropped were the *change in manufacturers' unfilled orders for durable goods*, and the *change in sensitive materials prices*.

The Historical Record

Most of the controversy concerning the index focuses on whether or not three consecutive downturns actually forecast an economic slowdown. Figure 2-7 below shows the revised Conference Board index where the shaded areas, as before, represent recessions so that we can compare the turning points of the index with real GDP contractions.

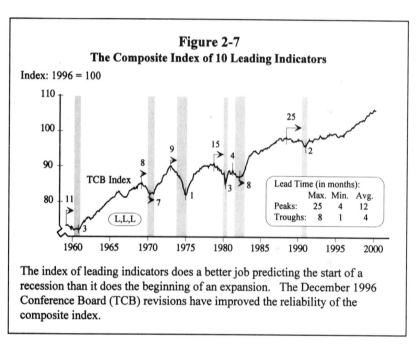

Figure 2-7
The Composite Index of 10 Leading Indicators

Index: 1996 = 100

The index of leading indicators does a better job predicting the start of a recession than it does the beginning of an expansion. The December 1996 Conference Board (TCB) revisions have improved the reliability of the composite index.

Figure 2-7 clearly shows that every recession during the last 40 years was preceded by a sharp drop in the composite index of leading indicators. The recession warnings given by the revised index averaged 12 months and ranged from 4 to 25 months.[17]

Less important, but worth mentioning, is the ability of the index to predict when a recession is about to end. Figure 2-7 shows that the lead time ranged from 1 to 8 months, with 4 being the average. However, because it takes several months or more to recognize a

---

[17] For the same period, the old BEA index averaged 13.1 months and ranged from 8-18 months. The Conference Board data in Figure 2-7 were initially released in December 1996.

turning point in the index, the economy is usually well out of the recession before the index can make the prediction.

Has the Index Ever Failed to Predict a Recession?

The older BEA index had a number of successes, along with a few false alarms. One was in 1966 when the index turned down for nine consecutive months and the economy still continued to grow. However, heavy (and to some extent hidden) spending on the Vietnam war may well have provided enough stimulus to avoid the recession.[18]

Another false prediction was in March 1984 when the index turned down for seven consecutive months. Critics pointed out that the index sent a strong signal, yet no recession followed. Advocates, however, argued that massive federal deficit spending—to the tune of $200 billion annually in 1985 and 1986—provided the same type of stimulus that the Vietnam war had earlier.

More recently, a series of declines in early 1995 presented another puzzling period for the leading index. At the time, it seemed that the index had peaked, but strong economic growth in 1996 suggests that 1995 was a relative, rather than an absolute, peak.

So, the short answer to our question is this: the old BEA index of 11 leading indicators predicted every single recession since 1955— along with a few that never occurred.

Did the Revisions Help?

Most economists seem to think so. In fact, the revisions resulted in three improvements. First, the size of the "false signal" in 1984 was muted. Second, the size of the 1989 downturn was more pronounced, giving a stronger warning of the impending recession. Third, the size of the false signal given in 1995 was reduced.

On the other hand, the historical data for the revised series still shows false warnings for mid-1966 and early 1995. Other revisions, such as the change to a 1996 base year, have no bearing on the turning points of the series.

---

18 Most economists exclude wartime periods because of distortion in the domestic statistics. The NBER, for example, compiles separate statistics on the length of peacetime expansions, contractions, and overall business cycles (see Table 2-2, page 22).

Are There Other Problems with the Index?

Frequent revisions of the monthly numbers are a major source of frustration. Whenever a new monthly composite index number is announced, revisions are also made to the six previous monthly numbers, primarily because the underlying individual component series are revised.

For example, suppose we have a period when the index has already turned down two months in a row. We anxiously await the next report, and it turns out to be another decline, but is coupled with an upward revision of an earlier (negative) number. This leaves us back where we started, with two *newer* consecutive months of decline—and our attention again riveted on the coming month's figures.

To make matters more interesting, some forecasters follow the individual component series that make up the composite index in hopes that they can forecast the change in the index that forecasts the change in the economy. As a result, the general direction of the leading index is usually known and can be forecast before the official numbers are released.

Despite some of these issues, the index of leading indicators is a popular forecasting device. It is one of the main tools in the forecaster's tool kit, and one of the most-watched statistical series in the economy today.

Index of Leading Indicators in Brief

Indicator status:	Leading for recessions, recoveries, and overall
Compiled by:	The Conference Board
Frequency:	Monthly
Release date:	4-5 weeks after the closing of the survey month
Revisions:	Up to six previous months are revised with every new release.
Published data:	*Business Cycle Indicators,* The Conference Board
Internet:	http://www.tcb-indicators.org
	http://www.EconSources.com
Hotline update:	(212)339-0330 for a recorded message 24 hours a day. The message is updated weekly to include new components as they become available.

Purchasing Managers' Index

One of the more interesting indicators of economic activity is the monthly *purchasing managers' index* (*PMI*) compiled by the National Association of Purchasing Management (NAPM).[19] Until recently, the series was one of a handful of major series maintained by a private industry and/or educational group rather than the U.S. Department of Commerce.[20]

The PMI is the major component of the NAPM's monthly Report on Business® which surveys manufacturing firms on a number of topics including production, new orders, inventories of purchased materials, employment, and supplier deliveries.[21] The NAPM releases the PMI on the first business day following the close of the reporting month.

The Sample and the Survey

The PMI is derived from a monthly survey of purchasing managers at over 300 companies in approximately 20 industries. Each industry is weighted according to its contribution to GDP, and each firm in the industry is given equal weight, regardless of its size.[22] The questions, such as the one following on supplier deliveries, are

---

[19] NAPM is a not-for-profit association that exists to educate, develop, and advance the purchasing and supply management profession. With more than 45,000 members, NAPM and its 180 affiliates works to establish and maintain best-in-class professional standards pertaining to research, education, and certification. For more information, contact NAPM Customer Service, P.O. Box 22160, Tempe AZ, 85285-2160, or call (480)752-6276.

[20] Other series examined in this book include the *help-wanted advertising index* and the *consumer confidence survey* compiled by The Conference Board, the *index of consumer expectations* compiled by the Institute for Social Research at the University of Michigan, the *Dow Jones Industrial Average* compiled by the Dow Jones Corporation, and the *S&P 500* by Standard & Poor's Corporation.

[21] The supplier deliveries series is used by The Conference Board as one of the components of its monthly *index of leading economic indicators*.

[22] Bretz, Robert J., "Behind the Economic Indicators of the NAPM Report on Business," July 1990, in NAPM's *Report on Business Information Kit*, March 2000.

unique in that they are designed to detect changes in the direction and intensity of business activity:[23]

> 9. SUPPLIER DELIVERIES - Check the **ONE** box that best expresses the current month's **OVERALL** delivery performance compared to the previous month.
>
> ☐ **Faster** than   ☐ **Same** as a   ☐ **Slower** than
>   a month ago   month ago   a month ago

When all of the responses are collected, the results are tabulated and then reported in the form of a diffusion index.

What Does a Diffusion Index Tell Us?

A diffusion index is different from other series in that it focuses on the direction and magnitude of change as opposed to the absolute level of the series. The index ranges from 0 to 100 percent and is considered to be expanding whenever it has a value greater than 50 percent, so the more the number exceeds 50 percent, the more intense the expansion of the series. By the same token, the series is contracting when the index is less than 50 percent—so the smaller the number, the more intense the contraction.[24]

In addition to the series on supplier deliveries, separate indices are constructed for production, new orders, inventories of purchased materials, and employment. These five series are combined to make up the overall purchasing management index.[25]

The Historical Record

Figure 2-8 shows the purchasing manager's index from 1959 through April, 2000. The horizontal line at 42.4 percent is the value of the index thought to be most consistent with no change in real GDP,

---

[23] Sample questionnaire, NAPM. NAPM calls the series "supplier deliveries;" BEA calls it "vendor performance."

[24] To illustrate, weights of 1, 0.5, and 0 are given to each of the three responses above. If half of the respondents select "faster" and if half respond "slower," the index will have a value of 50 percent [or, $0.5(1) + 0.5(0) = 0.5$]. Likewise, if 60 percent respond "faster," 20 percent "same," and 20 percent "slower," the index will have a value of 70 percent [or, $0.6(1) + 0.2(0.5) + 0.2(0) = 0.7$].

[25] The weights vary, with new orders having the most importance.

Figure 2-8
The Purchasing Managers' Index

Whenever the PMI is over 50 percent, the manufacturing sector of the economy is expanding. Whenever the PMI is greater than 42.4 percent, the overall economy—which includes services in addition to manufactured goods—is expanding. Because the PMI is a diffusion index, it has the properties of a leading indicator, reaching a peak before the economy peaks and a trough before the economy reaches a trough.

so the overall economy should expanding when the PMI is above 42.4, and contracting when the index is below it.[26] The manufacturing sector of the economy is also claimed to be generally expanding when the index is above 50 percent, and contracting when below that level.

According to the figure, the economy was expanding when the index exceeded 42.4 percent. At the same time, however, we should note that the index was in excess of 42.4 percent most of the time—including the majority of months during the 1970 and 1974 recessions. Accordingly, we have to be careful to avoid the use of simplistic rules when evaluating the series.

Instead, it helps to examine the intensity, or direction, of change as well as the general level of the index. For example, when the index

---

[26] This number is revised annually because GDP is continually being revised. When the last edition of this book was published in 1997, the number was 44.5 rather than 42.4, a relatively large change driven by the recent 1999 GDP benchmark revision. Most PMI changes, according to George McKittrick who does the annual revisions at the U.S. Department of Commerce, are relatively small, in the range of one or two tenths of a percent.

was above 42.4 percent and *rising*—the economy was indeed expanding. Yet, when the index was above 42.4 and *declining*—the economy was beginning to slow and occasionally even entered a recession.

The reason for this is that the PMI is a diffusion index, which means that it also has the properties of a leading indicator. If we examine Figure 2-8, we can see that the index peaked, with highly variable lead times, well in advance of every recession. Likewise, the index usually hit a minimum just before the recovery began. [27]

Since the BEA has never offered a leading or lagging classification for the series, we are left to our own judgments. Even so, it seems as if the peaks and troughs of the PMI function as highly variable leading indicators, while the level of the index tends to function more as a coincident indicator.[28]

The Purchasing Managers' Index in Brief

Indicator status:	The level of the PMI is a coincident indicator; peaks and troughs in the PMI series function more as leading indicators, with highly variable lead times
Compiled by:	National Association of Purchasing Management
Frequency:	Monthly
Release date:	First business day following close of the reporting month
Revisions:	None, responses are raw data and are not changed
Published data:	*Purchasing Today*, NAPM's monthly publication
Internet:	http://www.napm.org
	http://www.EconSources.com
Hotline update:	None

---

[27] The peak in the series is analogous to an inflection point in a series that grows first at an increasing and then at a decreasing rate. The trough is analogous to an inflection point for a series that decreases at an increasing and then at a decreasing rate.

[28] A 1985 paper presented by Theodore S. Torda at the NAPM International Conference and later published in *Purchasing Management* (July 1985, pp. 20-22) states that "... monthly data on the NAPM composite index and the Commerce Department's composite of leading economic indicators ... (both) tend to reach their peaks and troughs before those of the general business cycle." Later in the same paper, the author states that "the NAPM composite index clearly leads the (BEA) coincident index."

Another paper by Alan Raedels, "Forecasting the NAPM Purchasing Managers' Index," in the *Journal of Purchasing and Materials Management* (Fall 1990), concluded that "the Purchasing Manager's Index can be considered a coincident indicator of the economy."

Productivity

The key measure of efficiency in the U.S. economy is called *labor productivity* and it is published by the Bureau of Labor Statistics using quarterly GDP measures prepared by the Bureau of Economic Analysis. In fact, two series are released at the same time, one for the business sector and one for the nonfarm business sector. Because the data are based on quarterly GDP estimates, labor productivity is a quarterly series, although updates are issued monthly.

A third series reporting on manufacturing is also reported by the BLS, but it uses the industrial production indices compiled by the Federal Reserve System. As a result, there is usually a wide variation in the numbers reported at any given time.[29] The BLS business sector series is the most inclusive, but the nonfarm sector is also popular.

How Do We Measure Productivity?

The official BLS definition of business or labor productivity is as follows:

$$\text{Productivity} = \frac{\text{Index of real dollar output}}{\text{Hours of labor input}}$$

The numerator is based on, but is not exactly identical to, the GDP statistics in national income and product accounts, and is measured in real terms so that prices do not distort the dollar value of the output produced.[30] The denominator is obtained from the BLS Current Employment Statistics (CES) program which provides monthly employment data on payrolls in various industries.[31]

---

[29] In June 2000, the BLS reported revised first quarter productivity data of 1.8 percent for the business sector, 2.4 percent for the nonfarm business sector, and 7.3 percent for the manufacturing sector.

[30] For example, the outputs of general government, nonprofit institutions, paid employees of private households, and the rental value of owner-occupied dwellings are all excluded.

[31] *BLS Handbook of Methods,* Bulletin 2414, pp. 89-90.

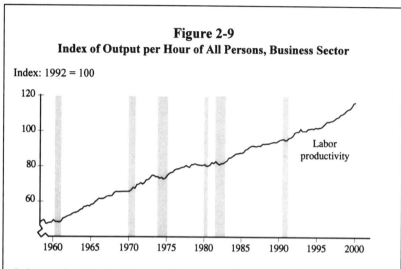

Figure 2-9
Index of Output per Hour of All Persons, Business Sector

Index: 1992 = 100

Labor productivity is defined as the amount of constant dollar output produced per hour of labor input. The level of productivity is an important economic measure, but not one well suited to short-term forecasting.

The Historical Record

The historical index, shown in Figure 2-9, indicates that productivity has grown slowly but steadily since the late 1950s. The index reached 116.6 in the first quarter of 2000, meaning that workers produced 16.6 percent more output per hour than they did in 1992. When farm workers are removed from the sample, the index changes to 116.3, indicating slightly lower productivity in manufacturing.

The index in the figure above appears to exhibit some cyclical behavior, with productivity falling off at the end of every expansion. Most economists think that this occurs because employers tend to hire less skilled and therefore less productive workers when production is high and unemployment rates are low. However, when productivity is expressed as a percentage change from the preceding quarter, as shown in Figure 2-10, it is evident that quarter-to-quarter changes are both volatile and generally unrelated to turning points in real GDP.

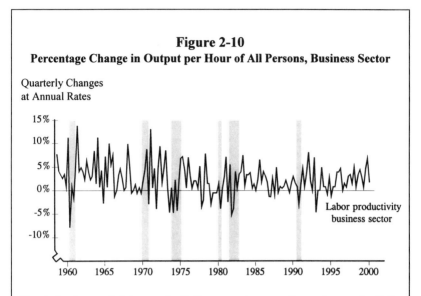

Figure 2-10

Percentage Change in Output per Hour of All Persons, Business Sector

Quarterly changes in labor productivity, a popular way of reporting productivity figures, can be quite dramatic from one quarter to the next. Productivity figures are best thought of as being related to long-term growth; they are unrelated to the turning points in the overall level of economic activity.

Multifactor Productivity

One of the drawbacks of labor productivity is that it ignores contributions by other factors of production such as capital. Most economists, for example, attribute the productivity growth spurt in the late 1990s to the use of the personal computer.

Accordingly, several *multifactor productivity* measures have been developed which relate output to a combination of inputs— including labor, capital, energy, and materials—that are used to produce that output. Unfortunately, some of the source data needed to construct such measures are not available quarterly, so the series are only compiled annually. Additionally, even the most recent data for the multifactor series are almost always several years old.[32]

---

[32] Even so, the BLS multifactor productivity web site at http://www.bls.gov/mprhome.htm allows you to retrieve annual multifactor productivity data as far back as 1949.

Labor Productivity in Perspective

The various labor productivity measures are extremely useful if we want to explain some of the factors that contribute to long-term economic growth. Quarterly productivity numbers, however, have little value as a forecasting tool.

If anything, the major problems with the series are in the measurement. For example, we already know that labor productivity ignores changes in the use of resources such as computers and other capital goods. Consequently, any change in the quantity or quality of other resources can make labor seem as if it is more productive than it really is.

Also, there are differences among the three main productivity measures because of the different series that are used in the numerator for each measure. The unfortunate result is that productivity measures are not directly comparable to one another, although each by itself gives a reasonable indication of long-term trends.

Finally, productivity numbers are slow to be reported because the series are constructed using quarterly data, especially those which come from the national income and product accounts. In essence, the quarterly output data must first be generated in order for productivity to be computed.

None of this is intended to disparage the series, of course, but we do need to know how the various series are measured if we are to interpret and use them properly.

Productivity in Brief	
Indicator status:	None
Compiled by:	Bureau of Labor Statistics
Frequency:	Quarterly
Release date:	about 40 days after the close of the quarter
Revisions:	First revisions 30 days after the initial release, additional final revision 60 days after initial release along with initial release of the next quarter estimates
Published Data:	*Monthly Labor Review*, U.S. Department of Labor *Economic Indicators*, Council of Economic Advisors
Internet:	http://stats.bls.gov/lprhome.htm http://www.EconSources.com
Hotline update:	202-691-5200

Capacity Utilization

When the Federal Reserve System collects data on industrial production, it also makes estimates of manufacturing capacity. When the Fed compares the level of industrial production to industrial or manufacturing capacity, the result is the *capacity utilization rate*. This monthly series is generally regarded as being a leading economic indicator for downturns in overall economic activity.

Measuring Capacity Utilization

The Fed's data on manufacturing capacity, like its *Index of Industrial Production*, are expressed in terms of an index with a base year of 1992 = 100. The former is then divided by the latter to express production as a percentage of actual capacity:

$$\text{Capacity Utilization Rate} = \frac{\text{Index of Industrial Production}}{\text{Index of Industrial Capacity}}$$

In January 2000, for example, the industrial production index stood at 141.5 while the capacity index stood at 173.3. When the former was divided by the latter, the capacity utilization rate was 81.6, or 81.6 percent.

Estimates of industrial capacity are available for a number of industries and product groups, including manufacturing, mining, utilities, durable goods, chemicals, and paper, to name a few. The monthly series is released approximately two weeks after the close of the month and is closely watched by many economists, especially those who watch the Fed.

Why Is Capacity Important to the Fed?

One of the responsibilities of the Fed is to foster steady economic growth in a climate of reasonable price stability. The capacity utilization rate is designed to tell the Fed if the economy is "heating up" to the point where inflation might surge because of production bottlenecks. This sometimes happens when demand for output is so strong that producers are tempted to use less skilled labor and less efficient equipment to generate even more output.

When the capacity utilization rate gets too high, the Fed might be tempted to tighten the money supply to slow the economy and lessen the threat of inflation. When the capacity utilization rate is lower, the economy is perceived to have some "slack" that acts to ease inflationary pressures.

What About the Historical Record?

The capacity utilization rates for two series, manufacturing and total industry, are shown in Figure 2-11. Because the series are expressed as a percent of capacity, their levels never exceed 100. Historically, the Bureau of Economic Analysis classified both as leading indicators for peaks (recessions), although the lead times are

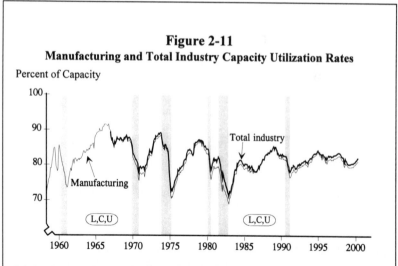

Figure 2-11
Manufacturing and Total Industry Capacity Utilization Rates

Originally, the Fed made capacity utilization estimates for manufacturing. Later, it added mining, utilities, and several others to get a "total industry" series which is now available from 1967 to the present. Despite the availability of the separate "total" series, manufacturing gets most of the attention.

too variable to be of precise value for forecasting. Overall, both series have unclassified indicator status.

The capacity utilization series, like most other economic data, are continually revised as new information becomes available and modifications in data collection and processing are introduced. Because capacity utilization is a ratio of two other series, a revision of either affects the ratio. Consequently, the monthly numbers are revised for up to three months, and the entire series is revised every Fall. Finally, a benchmark revision is conducted every five years.

This series is a little different from our other economic indicators in that it is not exclusively intended to forecast changes in future economic activity—but is instead designed as an aid to monetary policy.

Capacity Utilization in Brief

Indicator status:	Leading for recessions, coincident for recoveries
Compiled by:	Federal Reserve System Board of Governors
Frequency:	Monthly
Release date:	Preliminary estimate made midmonth of following month
Revisions:	The preliminary estimate is revised for up to 3 months; annual revisions are targeted for fall, benchmark revisions every 5 years
Published data:	*Economic Indicators*, Council of Economic Advisors *Federal Reserve Bulletin*, Fed Board of Governors *Statistical Release G.17*, Fed Board of Governors
Internet:	http://www.bog.frb.fed.us http://www.EconSources.com
Hotline Update:	None

Chapter 3

INVESTMENT AND CAPITAL EXPENDITURES

Gross Private Domestic Investment

In the first quarter of 2000, business investment expenditures, also known as *gross private domestic investment*, accounted for 17.6 percent of total GDP.[1] The majority of these expenditures were for nonresidential purposes—accounting for 12.9 percent of total GDP—with business equipment and software making up the largest part. Numerous series, indices, and other measures have been constructed to monitor these expenditures, but a subset called **gross private nonresidential fixed investment** is one of the most important.[2]

It turns out that this fixed investment series is generally coincident with changes in the direction of real GDP, so why is it so important? The answer is rooted in the long search for stable and predictable relationships in economics.

The Search for Stable Relationships

When Keynes wrote his magnificent *General Theory of Employment, Interest, and Money*[3] during the Great Depression of the 1930s, he offered a bold and radical explanation of how the economy

---

[1] From Table 2-3 on page 24 and Table 3-1 on page 51.

[2] Others are the *index of net business formation, number of new business incorporations, the index of industrial production—business equipment* (a subset of the Fed's *index of industrial production*), and several others covering contracts and orders.

[3] John Maynard Keynes, *The General Theory of Employment, Interest, and Money*, Harcourt, Brace & Co., New York, 1936.

functioned. His approach was based on a conceptual framework that broke the economy down into sectors and then described, in considerable detail, the spending behavior of each.

Among other things, Keynes argued that spending by the consumer sector was relatively stable. This was extremely important because if it could be shown that the greater part of total economic activity (later determined to be about two-thirds of total spending) behaved in a stable and predictable manner, the instability of the total economy must be due to other, and smaller, components.

Despite the fact that there were no existing GDP statistics that could be used to verify his convictions, Keynes' description of spending by each sector was so detailed that academicians started collecting data to test his theories. In the end, research largely confirmed the propositions put forth in the *General Theory*. Before long, the data grew into the NIPA accounts that feature the GDP, GNP, NNP, and other measures of aggregate economic performance that we use today.[4] These accounts, along with the organization of Tables 2-3 and 3-1, and numerous other tables and figures used throughout this book, are directly influenced by Keynes' work.

Table 3-1 illustrates the spending stability by the various sectors of the economy. The table follows the format of Table 2-3, only this time the focus is on quarterly percentage changes of GDP components over time. The first column shows the relative spending for each of the various categories in the first quarter of 2000; with consumers accounting for 68.2 percent of total expenditures, government and business each tied for second at 17.6 percent, and the foreign sector last with a net -3.5 percent. Columns 2 and 3 show the range of percentage changes for each category, with the average percentage change shown in the fourth column. The coefficient of variation, a measure of relative dispersion, appears in the last column.[5]

---

4 Simon Kuznets, the second American to win the Nobel Prize in economics, was already working on a set of national income accounts when Keynes was working on *The General Theory*. His data was used to test some of the theories put forth by Keynes

5 The coefficient of variation (CV) is the standard deviation divided by the mean—a measure that allows us to compare the variability of two series with different means. To illustrate, the CV of 0.42 for personal consumption expenditures tells us that quarterly percentage changes for this sector are one of the most stable in the table. A CV of 0.82 for gross private domestic investment means that quarterly percentage changes in this series are roughly 2 times (or .82/.42) more volatile than personal consumption expenditures.

Table 3-1

Quarterly Percentage Changes in GDP Components, 1958-2000

	% of GDP in 2000-I	Maximum Change	Minimum Change	Mean Change	CV
Gross domestic product	*100.0*	*5.9%*	*-1.6%*	*1.9%*	*0.50*
*Personal consumption expenditures**	*68.2*	*4.3%*	*-0.1%*	*1.9%*	*0.42*
Durable goods	8.5	12.9%	-9.2%	3.1%	0.72
Nondurable goods	20.2	4.1%	-0.7%	1.6%	0.54
Services	39.5	3.8%	0.8%	2.1%	0.30
Gross private domestic investment†	*17.6*	*15.0%*	*-14.5%*	*4.1%*	*0.82*
Fixed investment	17.3	9.2%	-6.9%	2.6%	0.67
Nonresidential	12.9	9.9%	-8.2%	2.7%	0.61
Residential	4.4	16.0%	-17.3%	3.9%	0.92
Change in private inventories	0.4	6,210.0%	-2,280.0%	188.7%	3.55
Net exports of goods and services‡	*-3.5*	*1,000.0%*	*-700.0%*	*63.7%*	*2.06*
Exports	10.8	21.5%	-10.9%	3.6%	0.94
Import	14.2	20.3%	-9.1%	3.7%	0.86
Govt. purchases of goods, services§	*17.6*	*4.9%*	*-1.7%*	*1.7%*	*0.62*
Federal	6.0	6.7%	-4.7%	1.9%	0.74
State and local	11.6	5.0%	-0.4%	2.0%	0.48

*Consumer sector   †Business sector
§Government sector   ‡Foreign Sector

Even the most casual inspection of the table reveals the stability of the consumer sector and the relative instability of the business (gross private domestic investment) sector that was predicted by Keynes.[6] This instability should be enough to make it worthy of study—but there's more. Investment sector expenditures, again as predicted by Keynes, have a way of causing *additional* expenditures through the multiplier principle.[7]

The multiplier works in both directions. On one hand, a reduction of investment spending would translate into an even larger reduction in overall spending, which Keynes felt was at least partially responsible for the Great Depression of the 1930s. On the other hand,

---

[6] The net foreign sector is the least stable of all, with a CV of 2.06, but it is also relatively small, and it was much smaller when Keynes published the *General Theory* in 1936.

[7] The multiplier is defined as the change in overall spending caused by a change in investment spending. The President's Council of Economic Advisors has estimated that the multiplier for the United States economy is about 2. This means that $1 billion of investment spending will ultimately generate $2 billion of total output.

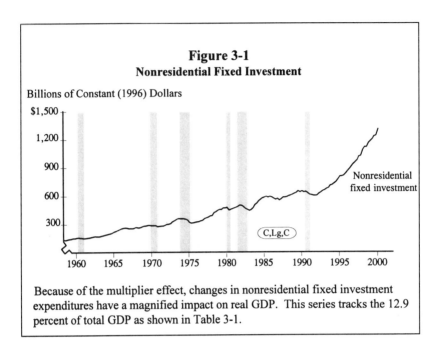

Figure 3-1
Nonresidential Fixed Investment

Billions of Constant (1996) Dollars

Because of the multiplier effect, changes in nonresidential fixed investment expenditures have a magnified impact on real GDP. This series tracks the 12.9 percent of total GDP as shown in Table 3-1.

"pump priming" in the form of additional federal government spending would have the opposite effect—causing even larger spending that would put the economy back on the track to recovery.

Looking Back – But Not Forward

The capital investment series plotted in Figure 3-1 gives us a feel for the instability of business sector spending. This instability is especially evident when the figure is compared to consumer spending such as that shown in Figure 5-1 on page 89. For example, nonresidential fixed investment in real or constant (1996) dollars peaked in the first quarter of 1990, and then dropped 9.4 percent over the next 8 quarters. During the same period, real (chained) dollar spending by the consumer sector dropped a scant 0.4 percent.

At one time, the government even kept a series on new or planned plant and equipment expenditures with data that was collected quarterly with a voluntary mail questionnaire sent out to a scientifically selected sample of firms in 39 industries. Eventually, however, the level of planned plant and equipment expenditures did not track well with the actual, and so it was dropped after the second quarter of 1994 in favor of a new semiannual series based on an Annual Capital Expenditures Survey (ACES).[8]

Unfortunately, these plans were then dropped for budgetary reasons even before any data were ever published. And so, despite the obvious importance of investment sector spending, and despite numerous monthly series that track specific investment sector categories, the federal government currently has no forward-looking series regarding planned capital expenditures.

The advantage of gross private nonresidential series is that it explains some of the observed variations in real GDP. The downside is that it, like many of the other NIPA components, is a quarterly report that that does a better job of telling us where we are, rather than where we are headed.

Gross Private Nonresidential Fixed Investment

Indicator status:	Coincident for recessions, lagging for recoveries, coincident overall
Compiled by:	Bureau of Economic Analysis
Frequency:	Quarterly
Release date:	End of the month with GDP revisions
Revisions:	Advance, revised, and final revisions along with GDP revisions
Published data:	*Economic Indicators*, Council of Economic Advisors *Survey of Current Business*, U.S. Department of Commerce
Internet:	http://www.bea.doc.gov http://www.EconSources.com
Hotline update:	(202)606-5306 as a component of GDP

---

[8] At the beginning of the year, firms would report their plans for first-quarter spending. If these plans were delayed, some respondents would simply push the planned expenditures ahead to the next quarter. When the last quarter arrived, however, there was a tendency for firms to simply cancel the delayed expenditures altogether, thus causing distortions in the quarterly figures. To make matters worse, benchmark revisions that were normally done every 5 years or so to assure the validity of the sample were not conducted after 1982. As a result, the series became less and less reliable with respect to the *level* of capital expenditures, although there was less concern with the timing of the turning points.

Building Permits and Housing Starts

Residential construction amounted to 4.4 percent of total GDP in the first quarter of 2000. This may not seem like a relatively large part of overall economic activity, but the multiplier effect causes housing expenditures to have an amplified impact on the economy. Several series are often used to track housing activity, but only the two that receive the most attention in the press will be discussed here: the number of new building permits issued, and statistics on the number of new homes started.[9]

The first is formally known as *new private housing units authorized by local building permits*—which explains the more common and considerably shorter title. Building permits is also the only housing series included in the composite *index of leading indicators*.[10] The second measure is the *new private housing units started* series. This differs from new building permits in that it represents actual home-building activity, not just the intention to build.[11] Both are monthly series that are released mid-month following the reference month.

Do Building Permits Predict Future Economic Activity?

On one level, the relationship between new building permits issued and overall economic activity may seem tenuous. In the first place, a building permit represents the *intention* to spend rather than

---

9 Two others are *gross private residential fixed investment* in constant dollars and the Department of Housing and Urban Development's (HUD) series on the sales of new homes. The former tracks the housing component of the NIPA accounts and is reported quarterly. The latter reports total dollar sales rather than thousands of units as is the case of housing starts.

10 The preliminary release, on a seasonally adjusted annual basis, is available on the twelfth workday of every month and is the one reported in the press. The final figures for the series are available on the eighteenth and are the ones included in the *index of leading indicators*.

11 Housing starts and building permits do not include mobile home units.

an actual commitment to spend.   The permit is also relatively inexpensive to obtain and is sometimes acquired partially for precautionary reasons, for example, "in case" the opportunity to build is right.   In addition, the amount of time between issuance of the permit and the start of the new residence may vary significantly from one location to another.

Finally, the intent to build may be adversely affected by changes in interest rates after the permit is issued.   In short, there are several reasons why the number of building permits issued might not work very well as an economic indicator.

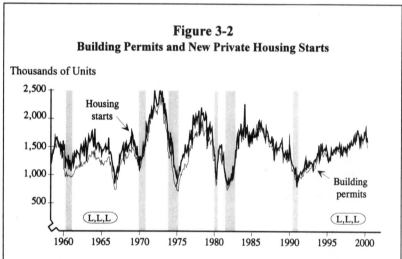

Figure 3-2
Building Permits and New Private Housing Starts

Thousands of Units

The number of new private housing (building) permits and new private housing units started both function as leading indicators for recessions and recoveries. The main problem with both series is the relative size of the month-to-month variations which can obscure the underlying trend.

The Historical Record

But, work well they do. As can be seen in Figure 3-2, the new private building permits series tends to increase sharply during the early years of an economic expansion and then decline sharply some months before the recession begins. Then, while the economy is in recession, the index tends to shoot up dramatically, foretelling the impending recovery.

A major problem, clearly evident in Figure 3-2, is the volatility of the series. Monthly double-digit changes are not infrequent, and a large changes in one direction are often followed by sharp reversals the very next month. To illustrate, building permits increased by 9.2 percent in January 2000, only to decline by 6.7 percent in February, and then fall again by 4.5 percent in March.

Some of the volatility is due to the nature of the industry, but some is also due to sampling variability. For example, the Census Bureau uses a mail survey to collect building permit data from local building permit officials. When requested reports are not received, missing values are simply estimated.

What About Housing Starts?

This series is similar to building permits in that it is expressed in terms of thousands of private houses started annually. It also exhibits similar volatility, but no more so than the building permits series.[12] To illustrate, in the first quarter of 2000, housing starts declined by 1.4 percent in January, rose by 3.6 percent in February, and then declined by 11.2 percent in March.

Weather is often the cause of such changes. Since builders usually have a backlog of building permits to use, they tend to break ground early when the weather permits and postpone starts when the weather is inclement—thereby causing housing starts to shift back and forth from one month to the next. Interest rates are another factor, especially in the first quarter of 2000 when the Fed was actively raising the discount rate in order to head off inflation.

Is One Preferable to the Other?

The good news is that both series function reasonably well as leading indicators for both peaks and troughs in overall economic

---

12 For the period shown in Figure 3-2, the average absolute monthly change (without regard to sign) in the building permits index was 4.6% percent, while the average monthly absolute change for new housing starts was 5.8% percent. The coefficient of variation (CV) was 0.94 for monthly changes in permits and 0.90 for monthly changes in starts, meaning that the two are generally comparable when it comes to volatility.

activity. As far as the peaks are concerned, Figure 3-2 clearly shows severe and protracted drops in both series just before the recessionary periods. The bad news is that both series are so volatile that monthly revisions often include changes in the *direction* of movement as well as magnitude. Because of this, the Census Bureau always shows the 90 percent confidence intervals along with the monthly percentage changes, although this is seldom reported in the press.[13]

The main problem with building permits and housing starts is one of interpretation: too often the focus seems to be on the size of the monthly change rather than on the underlying trend which may take several months to establish. Both series are revised extensively for several months after the preliminary release, so the trend can be established—it just takes a little longer.

Building Permits and Housing Starts in Brief

Indicator status:	Both series: leading for recessions and recoveries
Compiled by:	Bureau of the Census
Frequency:	Monthly
Release date:	Preliminary (both series): twelfth workday of the month
	Final (both series): eighteenth workday of the month
Revisions:	Building permits: previous two months revised monthly, annual revision every April
	Housing starts: previous two months revised monthly, annual revision every January
Published data:	*Housing Starts*, Bureau of the Census, U.S. Department of Commerce
	Economic Indicators, Council of Economic Advisors
Internet:	http://www.census.gov/indicator/www/housing.html
	http://www.EconSources.com
Hotline update:	Because building permits are a component of the *Index of Leading Indicators*, the brief leading indicator message at (212)339-0330 includes an update of the permits series when the composite index is updated.

---

[13] The March 2000 housing report stated that building permits for the first quarter of the year were down 2 percent, plus or minus 4 percent from the same period a year ago—indicating a 90 percent chance that the range would be from +2 percent to –6 percent. Whenever the confidence interval includes the value of 0, the change is not statistically significant—and so we are uncertain as to whether there actually was a decrease.

Business Inventories

Historically, inventories have played an important role in the literature on recessions and expansions.[14] In general, high inventories have been singled out as contributing to the cause of recessions, while low inventories are sometimes thought to be a sign that business activity is about to pick up. To see how this might come about, let's take a simplistic look at the process.

How Do Inventory Levels Affect Economic Activity?

First, it helps to think of inventories as being a buffer between production and sales. Now suppose that, for some reason, consumers cut back on their spending. The result is likely to be levels of unsold inventories in excess of what businesses would like to carry. If businesses react by reducing orders from suppliers, closing plants, and/or otherwise cutting back on manufacturing, workers will either work shorter hours or lose their jobs.

This, in turn, reduces the amount of income workers have to spend, which may actually cause inventory levels to *increase* again, rather than decrease as businesses had planned. If the cycle repeats itself, production will again fall, employment will dip, and consumer spending will drop, all of which may put the economy on the path to recession.

Eventually, businesses may succeed in reducing production to the point where inventories *are*, in fact, low. If they overshoot their mark, or if consumer spending increases even slightly, inventory shortages may develop. Businesses will then need to hire more

---

14 W.S. Jevons, Wesley Mitchell, and John Maynard Keynes were but a few of the many economists to incorporate the role of inventories into their view of the causes and explanations of economic fluctuations. In the late 1940s, Moses Abramovitz's classic work, *The Role of Inventories in Business Cycles*, was published by the National Bureau of Economic Research and did much to influence the way inventory statistics are compiled and reported today.

instead of fewer workers. This increases employment and consumer spending, causing inventories to go down again rather than up. As long as businesses continue to try to replenish inventories, the process of playing catch-up helps pull the economy out of recession and puts it on the path to recovery.

But Does It Really Work Like That?

The historical record may provide some clues. In Figure 3-3, the level of business inventories is plotted against aggregate economic activity.

Figure 3-3
The Level of Manufacturing and Trade Inventories

Monthly reports on the *level* of business inventories are often reported even though they tend to be lagging indicators which are of little value in predicting the direction of future economic activity. (Note: beginning in 1982, all inventory data were valued on a current cost basis, rather than at book values.)

Not very interesting, is it? In fact, any series that reports on the *level* of inventories usually tends to be more of a lagging, rather than a leading, indicator.[15] This is especially evident in Figure 3-3 above where inventory levels go up during the expansion and continue to rise

---

15 Another way to examine inventories is to construct an inventories to sales ratio. This series is covered in the next section.

right on into the recession. Eventually inventory levels may turn down, but not until the recession is about over.

Let's try again. This time (Figure 3-4) we will look at the *change* in the level of inventories rather than at the level itself.

Figure 3-4
The Monthly Change in Manufacturing Inventories

Monthly Percentage Changes

When we examine the *change* in inventories rather than the *level*, the series behaves more like a leading indicator. Because month-to-month fluctuations are so wide, a 6-month moving average can be used to smooth the series. Note that the series does not have to predict every single recession and expansion in order to be classified as a leading indicator—it just has to work most of the time.

That looks better! According to this series, the monthly percentage change in the level of inventories looks more like a leading indicator for recessions—with the series usually reaching a peak well before GDP turns down. The leading tendencies are more evident when a moving average is used to reduce the volatility, but the series is an improvement over the levels shown in Figure 3-3.

So Why Bother with Inventory Levels?

Because others do! In fact, many financial writers insist on reporting the level of business inventories (or a given subset) even though it is not helpful as an indicator of future economic activity. In addition, such reports often cite the series in current (inflation biased), not constant, dollars.[16] When this happens, the monthly series just goes up.

What Should We Remember About Inventory Statistics?

First, any series that reports *changes* in the level of inventories tends to act as a leading indicator for recessions and is therefore useful for forecasting changes in future economic activity. Unfortunately, monthly data such as that used in Figure 3-4 is in current dollars, which adds to the volatility. If we wanted an index that showed changes in real dollars, we would have to settle for quarterly data.

Second, for long-term analysis, the choice between monthly data and quarterly data is not critical because both are leading indicators for recessions and recoveries. Third, series that track inventory levels are not much help when forecasting future economic activity since they tend to act as lagging indicators.

Change in Manufacturing and Trade Inventories in Brief

Indicator status:	Leading indicator for recessions when *changes* in inventory levels are used; lagging for the actual levels themselves
Compiled by:	Bureau of Economic Analysis and Bureau of the Census
Frequency:	Monthly
Release date:	Second week of the following month
Revisions:	3 times every quarter as GDP is revised; annual revision in July for the previous 3 years
Published data:	*Economic Indicators*, Council of Economic Advisors *Manufacturing and Trade Inventories and Sales*, and *Survey of Current Business*, U.S. Department of Commerce
Internet:	http://www.census.gov/mtis/www/current.html http://www.EconSources.com
Hotline update:	(202)606-5306 for the quarterly *change in business inventories* data only

---

[16] The first release of numbers from any agency in the Department of Commerce is usually on a current dollar basis. This happens because the price index series used to convert current dollars to chain weighted (or real) dollars is not immediately available.

Inventory/Sales Ratios

Inventories may be a relatively small part of the overall economic picture, but their volatility is such that they attract more than their fair share of attention.[17] As a result, yet another way to examine the role of inventories is to combine them with sales in the form of a ratio. The Census Bureau compiles several ratios of inventories to sales, but the most comprehensive is the monthly **total business inventories/sales ratio** that appears approximately six weeks following the close of the reference month.[18]

Advantages of Ratios

Among the many advantages of ratios, two stand out. First, ratios can be constructed from other statistical series without actually having to collect new data. Second, ratios allow us to observe the interaction between two related series such as inventories and sales.

To illustrate, and in the absence of other information, it would be reasonable to assume that rising inventory levels would be a symptom of stable production and declining sales. If sales were actually increasing, however, sellers might well want to increase inventories in an effort to meet future demand. In this case, a simple ratio of inventories to sales might disclose a stable relationship between the two rather than a growing imbalance.

Leading Indicator Status

The proof, it is often said, "is in the pudding"—or in Figure 3-5 to be more exact. Specifically, it is evident that an inventory ratio is far more stable than monthly percentage changes in inventory levels.

---

17 Table 3-1 on page 51 illustrates both points. The change in private inventories during the first quarter of 2000 was less than one-half of one percent of total GDP, and the coefficient of variation indicates that it is the most volatile component of the GDP.

18 The main "total business" ratio is broken down into durable and nondurable goods for manufacturers, retailers, and merchant wholesalers.

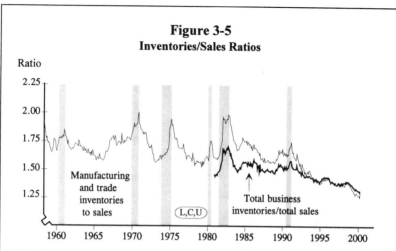

Figure 3-5
Inventories/Sales Ratios

Rising inventory levels may not be all that bad, especially if sales are rising even faster. As a result, the inventory/sales ratio is useful because it shows the relationship between the two related series. The ratio has considerable value as a leading indicator of future economic downturns.

The series also seems to behave much better as a leading indicator for recessions—turning up well before the recession arrives. Finally, we should note that our best and most comprehensive series is relatively new from a historical perspective. The "total business inventories" ratio shown in Figure 3-5 only goes back to 1981, so it only covers two of the six recessions since 1958. Even so, there is every reason to believe that it will perform as well as the older manufacturing series shown in the same figure.

Total Business Inventories/Sales Ratio

Indicator status:	Leading for peaks, coincident or unclassified otherwise
Compiled by:	Bureau of the Census
Frequency:	Monthly
Release date:	Mid-month following the reference month
Revisions:	Approximately 10 days after the initial mid-month release
Published data:	*Manufacturing and Trade Inventories and Sales NEWS* U.S. Department of Commerce
	Economic Indicators, Council of Economic Advisors
Internet:	http://census.gov/mtis/www/current.html
	http://www.EconSources.com
Hotline update:	none

Durable Goods Orders

Durable goods constitute such an important part of the overall economy, accounting for approximately 8 percent of total GDP, that separate statistics are often kept on this category.[19]   We must be careful to distinguish, however, between those durables that are intended for the consumer sector and those intended for use by the business sector.

The series called *manufacturers' new orders, durable goods industries* is a measure of the durable goods intended for the business sector.[20]   This statistic, representing about 4 percent of total GDP, is compiled monthly from survey data gathered from approximately 1,700 businesses and is released 3 weeks after the end of the month.

How Do Durable Goods *Orders* Differ from *Production*?

There are several important differences.   First, there is the difference in coverage mentioned above, with the series on durable goods orders representing a much smaller portion of GDP.   Second, the Federal Reserve System collects data on the production of all durable goods, whereas the Bureau of the Census, which is part of the Department of Commerce, collects the data on durable goods orders.

Third, data on durable goods orders are reported in billions of dollars rather than in the form of an index. Historical data is available in terms of real (chained) dollars, although the Census Bureau favors reports in the form of month-to-month percentage changes spanning 14-month periods—thereby avoiding the issue of choosing between current or constant dollar amounts. The historical measure is shown in Figure 3-5 to better illustrate the long-term trend.

---

19 From 1958 until the first quarter of 2000, spending on durable goods ranged from 7.0 to 9.5 percent of total GDP.

20 This series is often confused with another index, *manufacturers' new orders, consumer goods and materials industries,* which is one of the key components of the *index of leading indicators.*

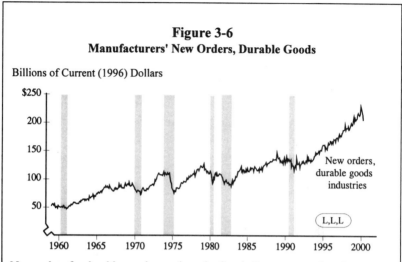

Figure 3-6
Manufacturers' New Orders, Durable Goods

Billions of Current (1996) Dollars

New orders,
durable goods
industries

L,L,L

New orders for durable goods may have leading indicator status, but the monthly numbers are so volatile that it is sometimes difficult to identify relative peaks and troughs. For the period shown in this figure, the monthly series declined 224 times and increased 270 times!

Just How Useful Is the Series?

Overall, the series gives an uneven performance as a leading indicator because it is so volatile from one month to the next. For the period covered in Figure 3-6, there were 224 monthly declines and 270 monthly increases. In the 106 months shown since the end of the 1990-1991 recession, the series even changed direction 77 times!

In addition to these frequent changes of direction, some of the monthly changes were quite dramatic. In December 1999, new orders for durable goods rose 6.5 percent, only to decline by a negative 1.9 in January 2000.

Whenever a statistical series exhibits this much volatility, it is difficult to infer much from the monthly changes. It is more useful when looked at over a longer period of time, and it may be better to use a moving average to smooth out the short-term changes.

Unfortunately, a large change in any statistical series can capture the attention of the press, and too much is often made of it. This is especially true when most of the other economic indicators are giving mixed signals—a combination of events that encourages people to look for more significance in a particular series than is warranted.

Overall, the durable goods orders series has historically performed as a leading indicator. It tends to peak before the economy peaks and to bottom out before the economy bottoms out. However, the variability of the lead times, along with the number and size of the monthly changes, means that this indicator of future economic activity should be used with caution.

New Durable Goods Orders in Brief

Indicator status:	Leading for recessions, recoveries, and overall economic activity
Compiled by:	Census Bureau
Frequency:	Monthly
Release date:	Third or fourth week following the end of the month
Revisions:	Monthly revisions to the beginning of the quarter, annual revisions in the Spring, benchmarks every 5 years
Published data:	*Economic Indicators*, Council of Economic Advisors
Internet:	http://www.census.gov/indicator/www/m3/index.htm
	http://www.EconSources.com
Hotline update:	None

Chapter 4

EMPLOYMENT, EARNINGS, AND PROFITS

The Unemployment Rate

Unemployment numbers, specifically those in the *civilian unemployment rate*, or simply the *unemployment rate*, are among the most widely watched of all economic statistics. The rate can move as much as one or two percentage points in a short time, but it has remained within a much smaller range since the Great Depression of the 1930s when it peaked at nearly 25 percent.

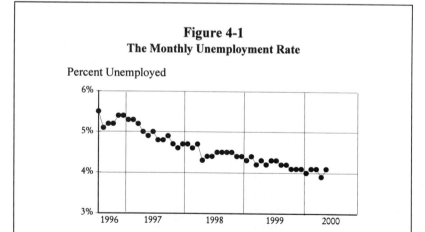

Figure 4-1
The Monthly Unemployment Rate

Percent Unemployed

In April 2000, the unemployment rate dropped to 3.9 percent, the lowest it has been since January 1971. Despite these relatively low numbers, every one-tenth of a percentage point represents slightly more than 141,000 unemployed people! In April 2000, there were approximately 5,524,000 unemployed individuals.

How Are the Data Collected?

Unemployment data are collected monthly by the Bureau of the Census for the Bureau of Labor Statistics (BLS) using a survey covering 50,000 households in approximately 2,000 counties and independent cities, with coverage in all 50 states and the District of Columbia. The survey is called the Current Population Survey (CPS), and it is the source of most labor market data, including earnings differentials among worker groups, labor force participation rates, and demographic characteristics of workers.

For consistency, the CPS is conducted in the week containing the 19th day of the month, with most questions relating to the week of the 12th day of the month. The BLS then compiles the data and usually issues labor force information on the first Friday of the following month.

The 1994 Current Population Survey Revision

From 1967 to 1993, the questionnaire for the CPS remained essentially unchanged. During that time, however, a number of changes in the economy such as the growth of service jobs, the decline of factory jobs, the growing role of women, and the proliferation of alternative work schedules, took place. As a result, a computer-automated questionnaire with slightly revised questions was introduced in 1994 in an effort to achieve more accurate results.

Under the old format, interviewers were equipped with a written list of questions, and the next question would be selected based on the answer to the previous question. Under the new format, each of the 1,500 Census Bureau interviewers use a portable computer that automatically selects the next question for them. The revised questions, shown in Figure 4-2, and the automated system generates more reliable results, but they also result in unemployment numbers that are about one-half a percentage higher than before. Consequently, the numbers we obtain today are not directly comparable to the ones obtained prior to 1994.[1]

---

[1] So, how can BLS claim that the 3.9 percent unemployment in April 2000 was the lowest since the early 1970s? The answer is that the rate reached 3.5 percent in December of 1969, and it was even as low as 3.4 percent in the first four months of the year. If the unemployment rate were to drop to 3.6 or 3.7 percent, then speculation might begin as to whether the numbers were the lowest since 1953, when it fell below 3 percent.

Figure 4-2
Current Population Survey – Selected Employment and Unemployment Questions

1. Does anyone in this household have a business or a farm?

2. LAST WEEK, did you do ANY work for (either) pay (or profit)?

   If 1 is "yes" and 2 is "no," ask 3.

3. LAST WEEK, did you do any unpaid work in the family business or farm?

   If 2 and 3 are both "no," ask 4.

4. LAST WEEK (in addition to the business), did you have a job, either full- or part-time? Include any job from which you were temporarily absent.

   If 4 is "no," ask 5.

5. LAST WEEK, were you on layoff from a job?

   If 5 is "yes," ask 6. If 5 is "no," ask 8.

6. Has your employer given you a date to return to work?

   If "no," ask 7.

7. Have you been given any indication that you will be recalled to work within the next 6 months?

   If "no," ask 8.

8. Have you been doing anything to find work during the last 4 weeks?

   If "yes," ask 9.

9. What are all of the things you have done to find work during the last 4 weeks?

Individuals are classified as employed if they say "yes" to questions 2, 3 (and work 15 hours or more in the reference week or receive profits from the business/farm), or 4.

Individuals available to work are classified as unemployed if they say "yes" to 5 and either 6 or 7, or if they say "yes" to 8 and provide a job search method that could have brought them into contact with a potential employer in 9.

Source: The questions above are from *Briefing Materials on the Redesigned Current Population Survey*, by the Bureau of Labor Statistics staff, February 4, 1994.

The Civilian Labor Force

One of the measures that comes out of the CPS is what economists call the *civilian labor force,* which consists of all civilians 16 years or older who are not confined to an institution. The term "civilian" is used to exclude members of the armed forces who make up a small, under two percent, but significant part of the labor force. Since members of the armed forces are always considered to be employed, the unemployment rate would tend to go down if we included several million people who all had jobs.

The part of the definition concerning the noninstitutional population is also intended to exclude those confined to a mental hospital or prison. After all, they can hardly be expected to be able to go out and seek, let alone hold, a job. Finally, the age limitation means that an enterprising 15-year-old working 50 hours a week cannot be counted as being either employed or unemployed—the person is simply defined as not being in the labor force.

What Does It Take To Be Employed?

Not much. Specifically, a person is classified as being employed if, during the reference week, he or she did any work at all as a paid employee; worked in their own business, profession, or on their own farm; or worked without pay at least 15 hours in a family business or farm. This means that a person who worked only one hour for pay during the reference week would be considered as being employed.

Since this may not seem very rigorous, what does it take to be considered unemployed? According to current definitions, a person would have to be out of work during the survey week, be available for work during the period, and have made a specific effort to find a job during the past month.

Have We Accounted for Everyone?

Not quite. Some individuals are marginally attached to the labor force. These are people who wanted to work, and were even available for work, but had stopped looking for jobs sometime during the past 12 months. Others are *discouraged workers* who have stopped looking for jobs specifically because they believed no jobs were available for them.[2] These people are neither employed nor unemployed—instead, they are simply not part of the labor force. In reality, marginally attached and discouraged workers are fairly common, especially during periods of recession or in areas where the number of homeless is quite high.

How Do We Get the Unemployment Rate?

This is the easy part. After we determine the number of unemployed persons, we divide them by the size of the civilian labor force. The April 2000 numbers looked like this:[3]

$$\text{Unemployment rate} = \frac{\text{number unemployed}}{\text{civilian labor force}} = \frac{5,524,000}{141,230,000} = 3.9\%$$

Since the monthly survey data also identify the unemployed by sex, race, age, and marital status, we could also get the unemployment rate for adult men, adult women, all teenagers, whites, blacks, black teenagers, and Hispanics. Unemployment rates for these groups are frequently reported along with the overall civilian unemployment rate.

Are Unemployment Numbers Really All That Significant?

More than you might imagine! Even a relatively small change in the monthly unemployment rate involves a large number of people. For example, with a civilian labor force of 141,230,000, an increase in the unemployment rate of just one-tenth of 1 percent would mean that an additional 141,230 individuals would be out of work. This is more than the total number of people currently living in New Haven, Connecticut, Lansing, Michigan, Topeka, Kansas, or Durham, North Carolina!

Incidentally, we might point out that the unemployment rate in the United States is measured differently than in many other nations. In the United States, we make an effort to look for the unemployed. In many other countries, people are not even counted as being unemployed until they actually show up to collect an unemployment

---

[2] April 2000, there were approximately 330,000 "discouraged workers."

[3] From BLS, *The Employment Situation: April 2000*, released May 5, 2000.

check—which results in the unemployment rate being understated in those nations.

What About the Historical Record?

The unemployment rates reached in early 2000 were some of the lowest ones achieved in nearly 50 years. The only time the rates have been lower was during the Korean war when it bottomed out at 2.5 percent.

One of the more interesting things is that the unemployment rate tends to vary considerably with the state of the economy. For example, whenever the economy is in a state of expansion (represented by the unshaded areas in Figure 4-3), the unemployment rate tends to fall—and somewhat slowly at that. However, when the economy is in a state of recession (represented by the shaded areas), the unemployment rate moves up rapidly. Indeed, one of the major concerns of economists is the speed at which the unemployment rate can climb. While the recent unemployment numbers in Figure 4-1

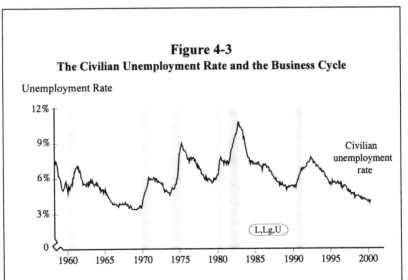

Figure 4-3
The Civilian Unemployment Rate and the Business Cycle

Unemployment Rate

L,Lg,U

Civilian unemployment rate

The unemployment rate acts like a leading indicator by turning up before a recession gets underway. Unfortunately, unemployment tends to increase fairly rapidly once a recession begins. After the recession is over, it usually takes several years for the rate to come back down to its former level.

look good, we should realize that (1) they are especially low from a historical viewpoint and (2) they are subject to sudden change.

Aside from the pain, suffering, and sheer waste of resources implicit in the index, the unemployment rate has some value as an indicator of future economic activity. Although the warning period is relatively short, the series tends to be a leading indicator of future economic downturns and a lagging indicator of impending recoveries.

Civilian Unemployment Rate in Brief

Indicator status:	Leading for recessions, lagging for recoveries, unclassified overall
Compiled by:	Bureau of Labor Statistics
Frequency:	Monthly
Release date:	Normally the first Friday of the following month
Revisions:	Monthly numbers not revised, annual revisions every January for the past 5 years to account for seasonal factors
Published data:	*Economic Indicators,* Council of Economic Advisors *Employment and Earnings,* Bureau of Labor Statistics
Internet:	http://www.bls.gov/eag/eag.us.htm http://www.EconSources.com
Hotline update:	(202)691-5200 for a short update on employment conditions, consumer prices, and producer prices

New Jobless Claims

The Employment and Training Administration (ETA) of the U.S. Department of Labor maintains an interesting cyclical indicator of employment and overall economic activity. Basically, new unemployment claims data are generated at the state level, and then collectively published as part of a combined federal/state program. The formal name of the series is *average weekly initial claims for state unemployment insurance* although it is more commonly called "new jobless claims."

The data are published weekly by the ETA in both seasonally adjusted and unadjusted formats. Because the weekly numbers are subject to such wide variations, a 4-week moving average is employed to smooth out the data. Figure 4-4 shows the movement of the smoothed series against the familiar recession-expansion background.

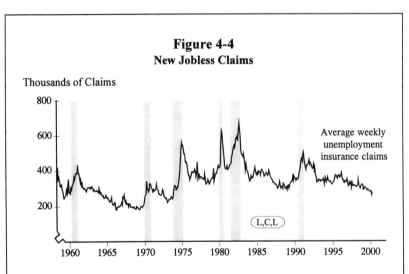

Figure 4-4
New Jobless Claims

Thousands of Claims

Average weekly unemployment insurance claims

New unemployment insurance claims are released weekly by the Department of Labor. Because unemployment claims often vary dramatically from one week to the next, a 4-week moving average is employed to smooth the data.

Are New Jobless Claims an Economic Indicator?

Since labor is a variable cost, meaning that the number of workers employed varies with changes in the level of production, new claims for unemployment insurance are intuitively appealing as an economic indicator.

Indeed, Figure 4-4 shows that new claims tend to decline during expansionary periods and then rise several months before the recession actually begins. This behavior makes the series a leading indicator when it comes to forecasting peaks in economic activity, a coincident indicator when it comes to predicting when the economy will bottom out, and a leading indicator overall. Because of the relatively uniform lead times for the turning points, The Conference Board includes the series as one of the *index of leading indicators* components.

Finally, a word of caution. The press often tends to report on individual weekly numbers rather than the moving average. Because these tend to vary so widely from one week to the next, the seasonally adjusted moving average is a much better measure of labor market conditions.[4]

New Jobless Claims in Brief

Indicator status:	Leading for recessions, coincident for recoveries, leading overall
Compiled by:	Employment and Training Administration, Dept of Labor
Frequency:	Weekly
Release date:	Second week following close of the latest reporting week
Revisions:	Previous 2 weeks revised with each weekly release, annual revisions in January for several years back
Published data:	*Economic Indicators*, Council of Economic Advisors *Weekly Unemployment Insurance Claims Report*, Employment and Training Administration, U.S. Department of Labor
Internet:	http://itsc.state.md.us http://www.EconSources.com
Hotline update:	(202)219-7388 for a brief recorded message

---

[4] Some states tie people's jobless payments to earnings in a base period such as the previous quarter. This often causes people to delay unemployment filings until a more favorable base period (one with less income) can be reported.

Help-Wanted Advertising

One of the handful of major statistics collected by a nongovernmental agency is the index of *help-wanted advertising in newspapers*. The monthly index is compiled by The Conference Board and is available from 1951 to the present with 1987 used as the base year.

How Is the Index Compiled?

The Conference Board collects data on the number of help-wanted classified ads printed in 51 cities around the country. In each city, a count of all classified ads is taken from a single newspaper, and the total is adjusted for both seasonal patterns and the number of days in each calendar month.[5] The count for each city is then weighted according to the size of the labor market in the region and, after some other minor adjustments, compiled and released. The index is available both in a "national" format, shown in Figure 4-5, and for each of nine census regions of the country.

What About Its Value as an Indicator?

In general, the monthly help-wanted index tends to be a fairly reliable leading indicator when it comes to predicting the end of an expansion. The index tends to peak several months before the recession sets in, and the amount of lead time is fairly consistent. It tends to fall throughout the recession and then bottom out just as, or shortly after, the recession ends. Finally, the data are normally not subject to revision, which means that we do not have to wait for additional data to see how a particular month fared.

Historically the BEA classified the index as a leading indicator for recessions and a lagging indicator for recoveries. This means that

---

5 See *The Help-Wanted Index: Technical Description and Behavioral Trends*, Conference Board Report No. 716.

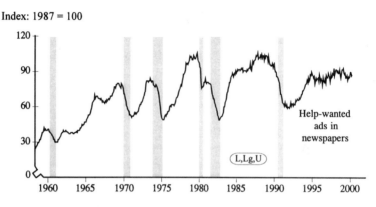

Figure 4-5
Help-Wanted Advertising in Newspapers

Index: 1987 = 100

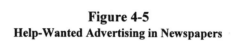

The Help-Wanted Advertising Index is based on the number of classified ads in 51 selected cities. Historically, the index has been a fairly reliable leading indicator of impending economic downturns.

the series has an overall rating as unclassified, but that does not diminish its value as a tool for predicting when the next recession might arrive.

Help-Wanted Advertising in Brief	
Indicator status:	Leading for recessions, lagging for recoveries, unclassified overall
Compiled by:	The Conference Board, 845 Third Avenue, New York, NY 10022
Frequency:	Monthly
Release date:	Approximately 4 weeks after the close of the reference month
Revisions:	Previous month's numbers not normally revised
Published data:	Monthly Conference Board press releases Conference Board Report No. 716
Internet:	http://www.tcb-indicators.org http://www.EconSources.com
Hotline update:	None

New Jobs Created

One so-called statistic is ***new jobs created***, usually stated in terms of the number of jobs created over period, such as a month or, in even numbered years, since the last election. Despite its widespread popularity, "new jobs created" is not a statistic at all. Neither the federal government nor any other group compiles this data.

The reason for this is that limitations in the source data makes the series difficult to compile on a regular basis. For example, the BLS estimates total employment from two data sources—a survey of business establishments and a survey of households conducted by the Bureau of the Census. The problem is that the total number of people employed, as reported by each survey, hardly ever matches because of multiple jobholders.

To illustrate, suppose you worked 20 hours a week at a department store and 17 hours a week at McBurger's. The business survey would reveal two jobs, but the household survey would only find one person employed. To reconcile the difference, the BLS simply combines the two and records one person as being employed 37 hours at the establishment where the most hours are worked.

Because part-time jobs have become so prevalent in our economy, total employment as measured by the survey of business establishments usually grows faster than employment measured by the household survey. It is this growth in the establishment survey that is usually—and mistakenly—cited as the source of the new jobs created "statistic." Of course, the title is catchy, and it is often used as a measure of a healthy and growing economy—which is why we hear about these new jobs created when we enter a new election cycle.

Finally, we should realize that bigger numbers (in this case more jobs) are not always better than smaller ones. After all, if you were to lose your job, and if you took two part-time ones in its place, the "new jobs created" series would go up.

Personal Income

Personal income sounds as if it should refer to the income people earn: their salaries, tips, and hourly wages. In a way it does, but in a more fundamental sense, ***personal income (PI)*** represents the total current income received by persons from all sources *minus* social insurance payments.

NIPA and Personal Income

GDP may be the primary measure of total output in the national income and product accounts, but it is not the best measure of the nation's income for two reasons. First, GDP *includes* output generated with resources owned by foreign residents. Since income earned by these individuals leaves the United States, it cannot be included as part of our nation's income. Second, GDP *ignores* income earned by U.S. residents as a result of their investments abroad.

Table 4-1
Converting GDP to GNP, Billions of Current Dollars

Gross domestic product (GDP)	**$9,697.6**
Plus: Income receipts earned abroad	337.2
Less: Income payments to foreign residents	379.7
Gross national product (GNP)	**9,655.1**

Preliminary estimates for 2000-I (totals may not add due to rounding)

Table 4-1 shows the two adjustments necessary to convert GDP (the measure of total domestic output) to GNP (the measure of total income).[6] The first step is to add the income earned by U.S. residents

---

[6] In the case of the U.S., the two adjustments are nearly offsetting, so that GNP and GDP are almost the same. This is not always the case for other countries. For example, Canada's GDP is several percentage points larger than its GNP because the foreign investment in Canada was much larger than Canadian investments in the rest of the world.

as a result of their international investments. The second step is to subtract the income earned by foreign residents as a result of their investments in the United States.[7]

The rest of the NIPA components are shown in Figure 4-6. To go from GNP to a ***net national product (NNP)*** of $8,471.1 billion, we subtract the wear and tear on the capital stock, more formally known as ***consumption of fixed capital***. The government then takes a slice of the income earned by businesses in the form of indirect business taxes,[8] and the remainder, called ***national income (NI)***, is $7,828.0 billion. This represents the sum of employee compensation, proprietors' income, rental income, corporate profits, and net interest payments in the economy.

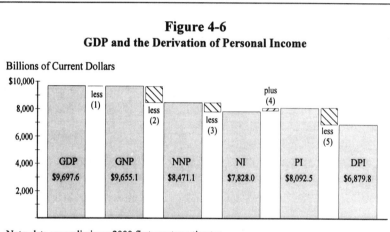

Figure 4-6
GDP and the Derivation of Personal Income

Note: data are preliminary 2000 first quarter estimates.
(1) Factor income payments to foreigners are subtracted, and factor income receipts from foreign residents are added to GDP to get gross national product (GNP).
(2) Consumption of fixed capital is subtracted from GNP to get net national product (NNP).
(3) Indirect business taxes are subtracted from NNP to get national income (NI).
(4) Undistributed corporate profits and social insurance payments are subtracted and transfer payments are added to NI to get personal income (PI).
(5) Tax and nontax payments are subtracted from PI to get disposable personal income (DPI).

---

[7] Because of these adjustments, it takes longer to obtain GNP estimates. Consequently, the GNP and other NIPA estimates in Table 4-1 and Figure 4-6 are *preliminary* first quarter estimates, whereas *advance* GDP estimates are shown in the tables on pages 24 and 51.

[8] Indirect taxes are the licenses, taxes, and other fees a firm pays to do business. Several other adjustments are also made at this stage, but the category of indirect business taxes is the most important.

To get to *personal income* (*PI*), undistributed corporate profits (retained earnings) and contributions for social insurance payments like social security are subtracted. At the same time, transfer payments, such as unemployment compensation, welfare, and other aid, are added in. The result, shown in Figure 4-6, is the aggregate measure called personal income in the amount of $8,092.5 billion.

Finally, if we subtract tax and other nontax payments from PI, we get a *disposable personal income* (*DPI*) of $6,879.8 billion, the income people actually have left over for spending purposes.

Now That We Have It, What Can We Do with It?

Plot it, naturally, and see what it looks like.

In Figure 4-6, personal income in both current and constant dollars is plotted against the familiar backdrop of business expansions and contractions.[9] As we can see, the trend in personal income when measured in current dollars seems to be up, regardless of the state of the economy. Indeed, 504 monthly statistics on PI are reported in the figure—and PI was down only 25 times (less than 5 percent of the total) during this entire period. Moreover, only 7 of the monthly declines took place during recessions—and there were no declines at all during the 1973 and 1981 recessions! As a result, a monthly decline of current dollar personal income may be newsworthy, but it may not be very meaningful.

A better measure is PI in real (chained) dollars which is not distorted by inflation. This series, also plotted in Figure 4-7, shows that personal income is flat to negative during recessions and generally up during expansions. In retrospect, this is exactly the pattern we should have expected. Personal income is such a large component of GDP (83.4 percent in the first quarter of 2000) that we would expect both to go up and down together—hence the coincident indicator status—even though the movements are relatively small. In fact, personal income would have been down a little more during the recessions had it not been for transfer payments which acted as buffers to cushion the decline in income.

---

[9] Personal income data is collected and published both monthly and quarterly. The monthly data is released in BEA's "Personal Income and Outlays" news release. Quarterly estimates for personal income are published in the *Survey of Current Business* along with other NIPA accounts.

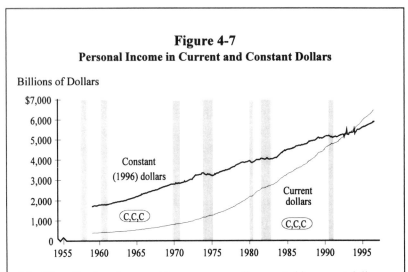

Figure 4-7
Personal Income in Current and Constant Dollars

Billions of Dollars

Monthly estimates of personal income are usually reported in current dollars simply because current dollar estimates are available first. Unfortunately, current dollar figures almost always go up, so they do not tell us as much either. Despite the brief delay in obtaining constant dollar figures, constant dollar measures are much more useful because they are not distorted by inflation.

On rare occasions PI can even be affected by political events. Right after the Presidential elections of 1992, many individuals who feared higher tax rates under the Clinton administration arranged to have their annual bonuses paid in December of 1992, rather than wait for January when a new tax year—and possibly higher tax rates— would apply.[10] This accounts for part of the $73 billion "spike" in PI that is so visible in Figure 4-7.

What Else Should We Know About Personal Income?

First, even though it is a coincident indicator, it has value because it tells us where we are and how we are doing. Coincident indicators just don't give us the advance warning of where the economy is heading that leading indicators do.

---

10 Under the Clinton administration, Congress made the individual income tax more progressive by adding a fourth marginal tax bracket of 39.6 percent which applied to taxable income over $250,000. The rates were also made retroactive to January 1993.

Also, we should note that because personal income is one of the national income and product account components, it is on the same revision schedule as GDP that was discussed earlier on page 18. As a result, any new monthly announcement of personal income will almost always mention a revision of the previous monthly figure.

A final issue is that the numbers for monthly personal income and disposable personal income are initially released in current, rather than real, dollar amounts. This is because the data needed to make the inflation adjustments are usually not available when the personal income figures are compiled. So while it may be quicker to release the data in current dollars, it has the unfortunate consequence of making the series appear to grow even faster than it actually does.

Personal Income, Disposable Personal Income in Brief

Indicator status:	Coincident for recessions and recoveries, coincident overall
Compiled by:	Bureau of Economic Analysis
Frequency:	Monthly
Release date:	End of month for the previous month
Revisions:	Preliminary and final revisions of the advance estimates
Published data:	*Economic Indicators*, Council of Economic Advisors
	Survey of Current Business, U.S. Department of Commerce
	Personal Income and Outlays, BEA News Release, U.S. Department of Commerce
Internet:	http://www.bea.doc.gov
	http://www.EconSources.com
Hotline update:	(202)606-5303 for a brief recorded message

Corporate Profits

The Bureau of Economic Analysis in the Department of Commerce compiles several series on corporate profits. Total profits are reported for domestic financial and nonfinancial firms, with the latter including estimates for manufacturing, trade, transportation and public utilities. The most important is *corporate profits after tax*.[11]

The Historical Record

We think of the net corporate profits series as being an indicator of the general financial health of the corporate sector. Indeed, this is exactly what the series is intended to measure, even if it does not receive the same lavish attention the press gives to the most recent

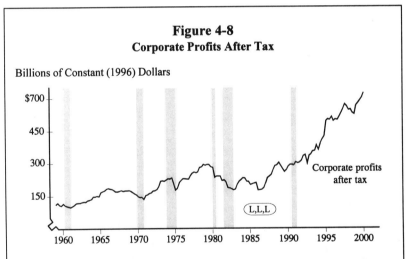

Figure 4-8
Corporate Profits After Tax

Billions of Constant (1996) Dollars

The most popular of the corporate profits series is the after-tax measure shown above. Because data are collected from quarterly corporate reports, the series is only available quarterly, and then after a considerable delay.

---

12 Other popular indicators, also leading indicators, are the *ratio, corporate profits after tax to corporate domestic income* and the *corporate net cash flow* series.

IBM, AT&T, or Microsoft earnings reports. The quarterly series is part of the GDP accounts and is released seven times a year, with the first release occurring approximately 45 days after the close of the quarter. The second is a final estimate which is based on more complete data and is released approximately 90 days after the close of the quarter.[12]

The leading indicator properties of corporate profits after tax are shown in Figure 4-8. In fact, with the exception of the 1973-74 recession, corporate profits have turned down well in advance of the general decline in economic activity.

Good, But Hard to Find

When we hear about "corporate profits" in the news, the reference frequently is to the quarterly earnings report of one or more individual companies—not the comprehensive series in Figure 4-8. Even so, the latter is far more inclusive, and gives us some indication as to the future movement of overall economic activity. As for its value to the casual observer, the main limitation is that it is buried in the GDP accounts, and it is reported on a somewhat irregular basis.

Corporate Profits in Brief	
Indicator status:	Leading indicator for recessions and recoveries, leading overall
Compiled by:	Bureau of Economic Analysis
Frequency:	Seven times a year
Release date:	Approximately 45 days following the close of the quarter
Revisions:	A second, final, revision appears 45 days after the first, or 90 days after the end of the quarter.
Published data:	*Economic Indicators,* Council of Economic Advisors *Survey of Current Business,* U.S. Department of Commerce
Internet:	http://www.bea.doc.gov http://www.EconSources.com
Hotline update:	(202)606-5306 for a brief recorded message when GDP updates are available

---

12 With the exception of the fourth quarter preliminary estimate, corporate profits are released along with the preliminary and final—but not the advance—GDP estimates. This means that the series is released seven times a year; three times with the preliminary GDP estimates, and four times with the final GDP estimates.

Chapter 5

SPENDING, SALES, AND EXPECTATIONS

Consumer Spending

Spending by consumers is often considered to be an important measure of the economy's health. Consumer spending is monitored by the U.S. Department of Commerce and is reported on a monthly basis in both current and constant (chained) dollars. As can be seen in Table 5-1, it is also the largest single component of GDP, accounting for more than two-thirds of all expenditures.

However, if you look in the Department of Commerce's index to current statistics, you won't find it listed under "consumer" or even "spending." Instead, it is called *personal consumption expenditures* and it is part of the national income and product accounts (NIPA).[1]

How Does Consumer Spending Behave?

It turns out that the category of personal consumption expenditures is the most stable component of the economy.[2] Because of its stability and because the initial release from the Department of Commerce is in current (rather than constant) dollars, the series generally tends to go up, regardless of whether the economy is expanding or not.

---

[1] This is not to be confused with the annual *consumer expenditures surveys* done by the Bureau of Labor Statistics which are designed to determine how individuals and households allocate their income among major spending categories such as food, housing, apparel, health care, entertainment, etc. The GDP accounts report consumer spending in terms of aggregates, not in average expenditures per unit.

[2] The reader may want to refer to Table 3-1 on page 51 to see how personal consumption expenditures varies with respect to other NIPA components.

To illustrate, 496 months of personal consumption expenditures are shown in Figure 5-1. During this period, the current dollar series turned down only 58 times—with 44 of the declines occurring during expansions and 14 occurring during recessions![3]

We get a better view of spending when the series is adjusted for inflation by using constant dollars, but even then spending is relatively stable. Real personal consumption expenditures turned down 5 of the 9 most recent recessionary months which began in July 1990, but the overall change in expenditures was negligible—amounting to less than one-half of one percent decline over the whole period.

Table 5-1
Personal Consumption Expenditures, Billions of Dollars

	Current	Constant (1996$)	% GDP
Gross domestic product	*$9,697.2*	*$9,156.6*	*100.0*
Personal consumption expenditures	*6,615.2*	*6,225.2*	*68.2*
Durable goods	825.5	898.1	8.5
Motor vehicles and parts	343.2	345.0	3.5
Furniture and household equipment	314.1	380.7	3.2
Other	168.2	175.0	1.7
Nondurable goods	1,963.3	1,842.4	20.2
Food	946.3	879.6	9.8
Clothing and shoes	324.6	338.6	3.3
Gasoline and oil	150.3	126.1	1.5
Fuel oil and coal	20.0	15.7	0.2
Other	522.0	483.5	5.4
Services	3,826.5	3,500.6	39.5
Housing	932.4	838.8	9.6
Household operation	369.5	364.6	3.8
Electricity and gas	131.7	132.1	1.4
Other household operations	237.8	232.2	2.5
Transportation	263.5	245.6	2.7
Medical care	978.1	895.4	10.1
Recreation	270.3	244.1	2.8
Other	1,012.7	911.0	10.4
Gross private domestic investment	*1,709.9*	*1,724.2*	*17.6*
Net exports of goods and services	*-335.0*	*-377.1*	*-3.5*
Government consumption & gross investment	*1,707.1*	*1,565.2*	*17.6*

Source: BEA News Release, first quarter 2000 (advance) estimates

[3] During this period, there were only four instances when monthly declines were back-to-back, and three of these were during recessions.

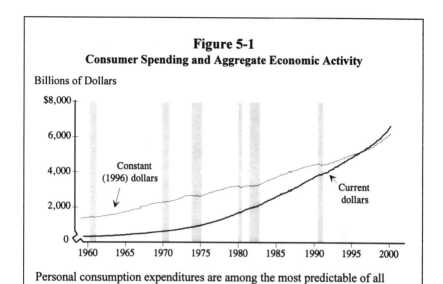

Figure 5-1
Consumer Spending and Aggregate Economic Activity

Billions of Dollars

Personal consumption expenditures are among the most predictable of all economic statistics, especially when measured in term of current dollars. A constant dollar measure gives a better picture of spending, but it too reflects the remarkable stability of consumer spending.

So, if personal consumption expenditures are so stable, and therefore so predictable, why do we hear so much about it?

Perhaps the reason is simply that the series is available. Of course, it's also so large that it is hard to ignore. The series does give us an idea of what is happening in the consumer sector, but it does not exhibit the type of behavior that helps us to predict changes in future economic activity.

Personal Consumption Expenditures in Brief	
Indicator status:	None
Compiled by:	Bureau of Economic Analysis
Frequency:	Monthly
Release date:	End of month on the day following release of GDP
Revisions:	Revisions of previous estimates to the beginning of the previous quarter
Published data:	*Survey of Current Business*, U.S. Department of Commerce
Internet:	http://www.bea.doc.gov/bea/rels.htm
	http://www.EconSources.com
Hotline update:	(202)606-5303 for personal income and outlays

Retail Sales

In order to collect data on retail sales, the Census Bureau conducts a monthly retail trade survey that covers approximately 12,000 firms. The first estimate of retail sales is published in a series called *advance monthly retail sales* and appears midmonth for the previous month. The series is revised two more times before the numbers become final, but the advance sales get the attention because they come out first. Breakdowns are available for a variety of industries, including building materials and hardware stores, automotive dealers, grocery stores, eating and drinking establishments, and many others.[4]

The Historical Record

This series is important because sales at retail outlets make up about 40 percent of the *personal consumption expenditures* series examined earlier. The advance release of monthly retail sales data is not adjusted for inflation, although constant dollar data are available shortly thereafter. In March 2000, the Census Bureau even released its first-ever report on retail E-commerce sales for the fourth quarter of 1999, but the series is too new to be of historical interest.

For the most part, the data reflect discretionary expenditures of the consumer sector, which accounts for some of the minor month-to-month variations evident in Figure 5-2, as well as some spending at retail establishments by governmental and business units. Even so, consumers often seem reluctant to reduce spending until they are forced to, which explains why retail sales in current dollars do not turn down until a recession begins. The reluctance to spend does not seem to last long, however, and before long consumer spending starts to pick

---

[4] The retail sales series is different from most NIPA data in that the monthly sales figures are not annualized. Instead, the monthly numbers report on sales for the period, and annual sales are determined by adding up the sales for each of the individual months. The series is, however, adjusted for seasonal, holiday, and trading day differences.

Figure 5-2
Monthly Retail Sales and Aggregate Economic Activity

Billions of Dollars

Total retail sales at stores

Approximately 40 percent of personal consumer expenditures takes place at retail stores. Some of the volatility of the series is due to big ticket items such as automobiles and furniture. The series behaves as a leading indicator when it comes to predicting the end of a recession.

up before the economy recovers, making the series a leading indicator for recoveries. This feature of the series is more clearly evident when the current dollar sales are converted to constant dollars, but current figures get most of the attention because they appear first.

Monthly Retail Sales in Brief	
Indicator status:	Leading for recoveries, unclassified otherwise
Compiled by:	Bureau of the Census
Frequency:	Monthly
Release date:	Approximately two weeks after the close of the month
Revisions:	Advance, preliminary, final estimates released at monthly intervals
Published data:	*Economic Indicators*, Council of Economic Advisors
	Advance Monthly Retail Sales, U.S. Department of Commerce
Internet:	http://www.census.gov/econ/www/retmenu.html
	http://www.EconSources.com
Hotline update:	None

Wholesale Sales

The monthly sales of merchant wholesalers, more commonly known as *monthly wholesale sales*, provide yet another view of aggregate economic activity. Unfortunately, the story they tell is not always clear because the numbers tend to move up and down on a fairly regular basis. Wholesale sales are about one-third the size of all manufacturing and trade sales.

Constructing the Survey

Monthly wholesale sales are derived from the monthly Wholesale Trade Survey conducted by the U.S. Census Bureau. The mail-out/mail-back survey covers approximately 7,100 wholesale firms that are primarily engaged in wholesale trade (jobbers, industrial distributors, exporters, importers, and others who take title to the goods they sell). Manufacturing firms that sell directly to the retailer, merchandise or commodity brokers, and merchants that work on commission are excluded.

The most recent figures are "preliminary" and are released about six weeks after the close of the reference month. "Final" figures are released at the same time for the month preceding the reference month. Finally, all of the series are revised annually, and benchmark revisions are carried out every few years.

Volatile Data is a Problem

One of the surprising things about the wholesale trade data is the high degree of variability in the monthly data. To illustrate, wholesale sales fell in 69 of the 208 months following the end of the 1982 recession—approximately one-third of the time—even though the economy was expanding for 200 of those same months. Volatility is even more of a problem over shorter time periods. According to the Census Bureau, the estimated median coefficient of variation—the standard deviation divided by the mean—ranged from a low of 1.4 for

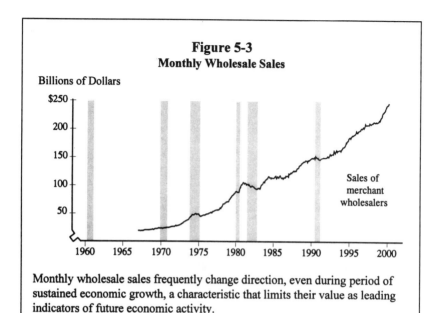

Figure 5-3
Monthly Wholesale Sales

Billions of Dollars

Sales of merchant wholesalers

Monthly wholesale sales frequently change direction, even during period of sustained economic growth, a characteristic that limits their value as leading indicators of future economic activity.

the whole index to as high as 7 for specific categories of goods.[5] As a result, changes in the level of wholesale sales have little value as indicators of future economic activity.

Monthly Wholesale Sales in Brief	
Indicator status:	No status with regard to future economic activity
Compiled by:	Bureau of the Census
Frequency:	Monthly
Release date:	Six weeks after the close of the reference month
Revisions:	Preliminary estimates are converted to final estimates after one month, annual revisions, benchmark revisions every few years.
Published data:	*Monthly Wholesale Trade*, Census Bureau
	Economic Indicators, Council of Economic Advisors
Internet:	http://www.census.gov/svsd/www/mwts.html
	http://www.EconSources.com
Hotline update:	none

[5] From the *Current Wholesale Report*, Table 3. Estimated Coefficients of Variation of Monthly Sales and End-of-Month Inventories, May 5, 2000.

Employment Cost Index

The quarterly *employment cost index* (ECI) is a relatively new series that is designed to measure the change in the cost of labor over time. The series includes wages, salaries, and the employer's cost of employee benefits. The measure dates from 1982, and it has a wide following, even though it is only reported quarterly.

Like most other series, we can focus on the level of the index, or changes in the level. The most popular version, shown in Figure 5-4, is in terms of percentage changes of quarterly data, although percentage changes over 12-month periods are also available.

Uses and Users of the ECI

Because the ECI reflects employment cost trends, and because the cost of labor is such a large component of production, it is often used in escalator clauses. The federal government uses the series to adjust defense contracts, and it is even used to determine allowable increases in Medicare hospital charges.

The series is also used in numerous private and public sector collective bargaining agreements—including the District of Columbia, Baltimore, and Los Angeles. Federal pay adjustments for the U.S. Congress, federal judges, and senior government officials are also tied to the ECI, as are the salaries of officials in a number of states.

Finally, the Federal Reserve System uses the ECI as an indicator of future inflation—as a way to predict where we are headed, rather than to tell us where we have been. In fact, the Fed seldom raises the discount rate without voicing some concern over increases in current or expected future labor costs.

The National Compensation Survey

The ECI is a series in transition as it is currently in the process of being merged into a broader national compensation (NCS) survey.

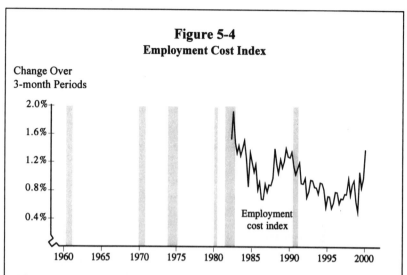

Figure 5-4
Employment Cost Index

The employment cost index, available only since 1982, is used as an escalator to adjust national defense contracts and federal pay scales. It is thought to be an indicator of future inflation and is closely watched by the Fed. It has no properties as an indicator of future changes in aggregate economic activity.

The new NCS series is designed to replace three overlapping series that provide a broad range of information on employee salaries, wages and benefits.[6] Because of the popularity of the ECI, however, it is likely that much of the data will be continued.

Employment Cost Index in Brief	
Indicator status:	No status with regard to future economic activity
Compiled by:	Bureau of Labor Statistics
Frequency:	Quarterly
Release date:	End of the month following the reference quarter
Revisions:	To be revised as part of the National Compensation Survey
Published data:	*BLS News–Employment Cost Index,* Dept of Labor
	Economic Indicators, Council of Economic Advisors
Internet:	http://stats.bls.gov/ecthome.htm
	http://www.EconSources.com
Hotline update:	None

---

[6] The NCS will have a much broader coverage, expanding the number of establishments surveyed from approximately 6,000 to 36,000.

Consumer Expectations and Confidence

Because the consumer sector makes up such a large portion of the overall economy, it is reasonable to assume that people's decisions to save or spend can be affected by the expectations and confidence they have in the economy. Both considerations are important, and two highly regarded series are designed to track these factors.

Consumer Expectations

The first of the two series is derived from a "consumer sentiment" survey compiled by the Institute for Social Research (ISR) at the University of Michigan. The survey is based on a random monthly sample of 500 people selected from all states except Alaska and Hawaii. The sample is closed, which means that only the individuals initially selected for the sample are contacted for the survey. Because of the design, a new group of consumers appears in the sample every month.[7]

The survey covers five major categories reported as separate indices: personal finance, current and expected; business conditions, current and expected; and buying conditions. The results of the survey are compiled and made available for release no later than the first week of the following month.[8]

One of the subcomponents of the survey is the *index of consumer expectations* shown in Figure 5-4. Historically the index

---

[7] According to Richard T. Curtin at the Survey Research Center, "The sample is designed to maximize the study of change by incorporating a rotating panel sample design in an ongoing monthly survey program. For each monthly sample, an independent cross-section sample of households is drawn. The respondents chosen in this drawing are then reinterviewed six months later. A rotating panel design results, and the total sample for any one survey is normally made up of 55% new respondent, and 45% being reviewed for the second time." *Surveys of Consumers*, Survey Research Center.

[8] The monthly reports are available on a subscription basis. For further information contact Surveys of Consumers, Survey Research Center, University of Michigan, 426 Thompson Street, Ann Arbor, MI, 48104-2321.

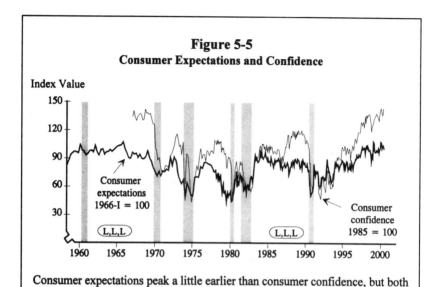

Figure 5-5
Consumer Expectations and Confidence

Consumer expectations peak a little earlier than consumer confidence, but both function well as leading economic indicators. The longer series prepared by the ISR at Michigan is one of the *index of leading indicator* components.

performed so well as a leading indicator of future economic activity that it was included as one of the individual components in The Conference Board's composite *index of leading indicators*.

Consumer Confidence

In 1967, The Conference Board introduced its **consumer confidence survey**.[9] This survey takes place during the first 2 weeks of every month and covers 5,000 households. Data are then compiled and released during the first week of the following month.

Consumer confidence is expressed as an index with a base of 1985=100, and it covers a number of categories, including appraisals of the current business situation; expectations of business conditions, employment, and income for the next six months; plans to buy automobiles, homes, and major appliances in the next six months; and questions on vacation plans. The index is available ona regional basis

---

[9] See the *Consumer Confidence Survey*, a monthly report from the Consumer Research Center, The Conference Board, 845 Third Ave, New York, NY 10022. The Conference Board also compiles the *index of leading indicators*.

and is also broken down by age of household head and by household income.

Looking Ahead

Both series are important leading indicators, turning down before the economy peaks, and turning up before the economy recovers. If anything, the index of consumer expectations tends to peak somewhat earlier than the confidence measure, and it tends to recover somewhat earlier as well. Both series are widely followed, and both are used to forecast impending economic developments.

Perhaps the most importance difference between the two series is accessibility. Both series are available on a subscription basis to users, but only The Conference Board issues monthly press releases with the latest numbers.[10] As a result, the monthly numbers we hear about in the press are The Conference Board's consumer confidence series.

Consumer Expectations and Confidence	
Indicator status:	Both series are leading for recessions and recoveries
Compiled by:	*Consumer Confidence,* The Conference Board
	Consumer Expectations, Institute for Social Research, University of Michigan
Frequency:	Monthly (both)
Release date:	First week of following month (both)
Published data:	*Consumer Confidence Survey,* subscription from The Conference Board
	Consumer Expectations, subscription basis from ISR
Internet:	http://www.conference-board.org
	http://www.isr.umich.edu/src/
	http://www.EconSources.com
Hotline update:	(212)339-0330 for updates of *consumer expectations* as Updates to the *index of leading indicators* become available

10 The monthly number for consumer expectations is normally available from The Conference Board on its leading economic indicator telephone hotline. Otherwise, the data on the ISR website is several months old.

The Beige Book

There are a number of economic statistics that affect our daily lives. Most, like GDP, industrial production, and the unemployment rate, are statistics in the true sense of the word. Others, like "new jobs created," are not statistics at all, although they are often reported as if they really were.

The Beige Book, the summary of economic conditions and collection of anecdotal information that is prepared by the Fed, fits into this category. The report is released eight times a year, and— because it appears two weeks prior to the Fed's monetary policy meetings—it is often treated as if it were a guide to what the Fed intends to do. The reality is much different.

The Demise of Discretionary Fiscal Policy

Discretionary fiscal policy, our federal government's taxing and spending behavior, has become so politically driven and so cumbersome in its application that it cannot respond very effectively to rapid changes in economic conditions. As a result, we rely more on programs that are more or less fixed, such as progressive income tax rates, unemployment insurance compensation, welfare subsidies, and other such programs that economists call automatic stabilizers.

The fiscal policy gridlock has, in effect, allowed discretionary economic policy-making to become the virtual prerogative of the Fed. This development is also largely responsible for spawning the many "Fed watchers" among us.

The Fed and Monetary Policy

Trying to get a handle on what is going to happen in the American economy today is often considered largely synonymous with trying to figure out what the Federal Reserve System is going to do. However, the execution of monetary policy is the easy part because the Fed only has to increase or decrease the size of the money supply in order to affect the availability and cost of credit. The laws of supply and demand reign supreme here: increase the money supply, and interest rates go down, reduce or tighten the money supply, and rates go up.[11]

Monetary Policy Decision Variables

The hard part of monetary policy is to decide which way to go, as in the first half of 2000 when the Fed though it was confronted with a choice between controlling future inflation (and jeopardizing the all-time record expansion that began in 1991), or of allowing economic events to take their course (and risking higher inflation later on).

The policy makers at the Fed certainly watch all of the statistics explored in this book, but they also want to know as much as possible about other economic conditions that are more difficult to quantify. Besides, the Fed has a long tradition of considering the regional viewpoints of its twelve district banks before it makes its monetary policy decisions. As a result, by 1970 these regional summaries were formalized in a confidential—for policymakers only—report called *The Red Book*.[12]

By the early 1980s, however, Congress was pressing the Fed to be more open with respect to its monetary policy making. The result was the release of *The Red Book* to the public in 1983. To mark this change, the cover of the report was changed to beige, hence what is known today as *The Beige Book*.

The modern report is approximately 30 pages long and draws on a variety of information from the board of directors at the Fed's twelve district banks, branch bank directors, contacts in the business community, and so on. A summary of national economic conditions, shown in Figure 5-6, makes up the first part of *The Beige Book*. Summaries of economic conditions in each of the twelve districts make up the remainder. There are no statistical tables in the report.

---

[11] Assuming *ceteris paribus* of course, the assumption that all other things remain constant while the money supply changes.

[12] See Fettig, Rolnick, and Runkle, "The Federal Reserve's Beige Book, A Better Mirror than Crystal Ball," *The Region*, Federal Reserve Bank of Minneapolis, March 1999, for an excellent history and summary (the article can be retrieved from either of the two web sites listed at the end of this section).

Figure 5-6
The Beige Book – Summary of Commentary of
Current Economic Conditions by Federal Reserve District

Reports from the twelve Federal Reserve Districts indicated that the economy continued to expand during March and the first three weeks of April. The majority of Districts reported moderate to strong economic growth, with only Richmond and Chicago noting some signs that overall growth had slowed slightly. Consumer spending was strong and retail sales were in line with most merchants' expectations. Commercial construction activity generally remained robust, while several Districts noted softening demand on the residential side. Factories were running near capacity in some areas, as overall manufacturing activity was strong. Dry soil conditions were reported in many areas, but spring planting proceeded at a rapid pace. Oil drilling activity was up from a year ago.

There were more frequent reports of intensifying wage pressures as shortages of workers persisted in all Districts. Increasing input prices were noted in nearly every region. Many Districts cited wider use of fuel surcharges by shipping firms and other transportation companies. Manufacturers in several areas also reported higher prices for petroleum-related inputs, such as rubber and plastics, as well as for some nonpetroleum-related inputs. However, there were only a few reports that increases in input costs were resulting in higher prices at the retail level.

District reports generally indicated that recent volatility in equity markets had not had an impact on activity as of the time of this report, although it had altered some contacts' expectations.

The above *Beige Book* summary was prepared by the Federal Reserve Bank of Chicago and was made public two weeks prior to the May monetary policy meeting. The Fed cautions that the Beige Book comments are commentaries only, and not the official views of the Fed.

Source: *Beige Book*, May 3, 2000

The summary in Figure 5-6 goes on to describe conditions in the areas of consumer spending, real estate and construction, manufacturing, banking and finance, labor markets, and agriculture and natural resources. If that doesn't leave you bleary-eyed, you can pursue 25 more pages of similar commentary at the regional level.[13]

---

[13] We have never, in fact, met a single living economist outside the Fed who has read any of the *Beige Books* from beginning to end.

Mirror or Crystal Ball?

The question facing Fed watchers is the extent to which the Beige Book reflects actual conditions in the economy, or, alternatively, provides us with an insight into the Fed's likely intentions. Do statements such as "There were more frequent reports of intensifying wage pressures as shortages of workers persisted in all Districts" mean that the Fed will proceed to raise interest rates?

Fed economists have tried to answer this question by assigning numerical scores to various aspects of more than 260 *Beige Books* published since 1970. The scores were then analyzed to see if they could improve on the estimates given by the computerized forecasting models already used by the Fed. One study found that *The Beige Book* was of some help. Another, and more complete, study found that a close examination of the *Beige Book* could not improve on the quality of output already provided by private sector forecasts. According to the latter, "the media and Fed watchers would do well to put aside *The Beige Book* and focus on private sector forecasts in their attempts to predict monetary policy."[14]

So, why bother with *The Beige Book*? For one, any given report is quite detailed and generally covers important regional developments in the retail trades, labor markets, agricultural outlook, industrial production, and so on: just the kinds of things that are not always well revealed by statistics. For another, we hear about it in the press often enough to realize that we should know more about it. Finally, it is nice to know some of what the Fed knows—even if the product is more of a mirror than a crystal ball.

The Beige Book in Brief	
Indicator status:	None
Compiled by:	The Federal Reserve Bank of Chicago
Frequency:	Eight times per year
Release date:	Two weeks preceding the Fed's FOMC meeting
Published data:	*The Beige Book*, The Federal Reserve Board of Governors
Internet:	http://www.federalreserve.gov/policy.htm
	http://www.EconSources.com
Hotline update:	none

---

[14] Fettig, et al. "The Federal Reserve's Beige Book," *The Region*, 1999. This article describes both studies in more detail.

Chapter 6

PRICES, MONEY, AND INTEREST RATES

The Consumer Price Index

The consumer price index, or CPI, is one of the most comprehensive statistical measures compiled by the Bureau of Labor Statistics. In fact, the BLS actually computes two measures. The first, and most important, is the *CPI for all urban consumers (CPI-U)*, which covers about 87 percent of the total population. The second, which overlaps the first, is the *CPI for urban wage earners and clerical workers (CPI-W)* and covers about 32 percent of the population. CPI data are released about two weeks after the close of the reference month.

Each index is a measure of the average change in prices for a fixed "market basket" of goods and services used by consumers. It is not, however, the same as a cost-of-living index because it does not take into account all of the factors that would allow one to maintain the same standard of living with a given level of expenditures.[1]

Constructing the Sample

The CPI uses a market basket of goods and services that consumers typically bought during a 1993-95 base period. From this,

---

[1] Missing from the analysis are such things as the impact of government regulations on our lives, environmental factors, even things like crime, health, and water quality. When asked by a Congressional advisory committee to establish a cost of living index as the primary objective of the CPI, the BLS response was that "if the BLS staff or other technical experts knew how to produce a true cost-or-living index on a monthly production schedule, that would be what we would produce." See "Consumer Price Indexes: Short Term Recommendations," on the 1998 CPI Revisions BLS web site.

the BLS constructed a list of eight major product groups (PGs) which were broken down into approximately 70 expenditure classes (ECs), nearly 200 strata, and approximately 400 entry level items (ELIs) in the manner illustrated in Figure 6-1. Approximately 80,000 individual products were then selected as being representative ELI category items.

Table 6-1
Major Product Groups and Entry Level Sampling Items in the CPI

PG#1. Food and Beverages
    EC#1: Cereals and Bakery Products
        Strata #1: Cereals and cereal products
            ELI#1: *Flour and prepared flour mixes*
            ELI#2: *Breakfast cereal*
            ELI#3: *Rice, Pasta, and corn meal*
        Strata #2: Bakery products
            ELI#1: *White Bread*
            ELI#2: *Other Bread*
        Strata #3: Fresh biscuits, rolls, muffins
PG#2. Housing
PG#3. Apparel
PG#4. Transportation
PG#5. Medical Care
PG#6. Recreation
PG#7. Education and Communication
PG#8. Other Goods and Services

Each of these 80,000 items are then priced and repriced all over again at regular monthly intervals. Because the final dollar value of an 80,000 item market basket would be so large, however, the new market basket prices are expressed as a percent of the base period prices.

To illustrate, when the CPI reached 171.1 in March 2000, it meant that the total market basket amounted to 171.1 percent of its base period cost, or that a typical item costing $1 in the base period cost $1.71 in March 2000. Market baskets are typically revised every 10 years or so, and the base year index is usually updated whenever the market basket is updated. However, the CPI is one of the few exceptions to this rule largely because so many CPI users were so familiar with, and had extensive records of, prices with the 1982-84 base period. As a result, new prices are reported as a percent of their 1982-84 base, while the market basket items that make up the sample are based on 1993-95 consumer expenditure patterns.[2]

Estimating Inflation from the CPI

Because the CPI measures the level of prices, it does not directly measure inflation. However, inflation estimates can be derived by computing the change in the level of the CPI from one period to another. The one we hear about most often is based on 1-month percentage changes in the CPI-U that are adjusted for seasonal variations and then annualized. Consumer prices are also reported for various other categories such as food and energy.

However, annualized estimates based on 1-month changes often result in relatively wide swings in the inflation rate, so it is generally preferable to compute the change over longer periods such as the 3-month spans shown in Figure 6-2. Another measure is the so-called "core" rate of inflation which does not include the more volatile food and energy price categories. The historical record shows that inflation tends to get worse in the latter stages of an expansion, but other than that, inflation has no value as an indicator of future economic activity.

Other Uses for the CPI

Even though the CPI is not a cost of living measure, it is often used as a surrogate. According to the BLS, the CPI affects the income of about 70 million persons: over 43 million social security beneficiaries, nearly 22 million food stamp recipients, and approximately 4 million military and Federal Civil Service retirees and survivors. It is also used in escalator clauses for about 3 million workers covered by collective bargaining agreements. Changes in the CPI also affect more than 24 million children who eat school lunches, as well as the annual Federal income tax bracket adjustments.

---

[2] The choice of a base year is not that important because comparisons between any two years can be found by simply dividing two values of the CPI. If the CPI in March 2000 was 171.1, and if the CPI in March 1999 was 165.1, then March 2000 prices were 171.1/165.1 = 1.036, or 1.036 times higher than they were a year earlier. Alternatively, we could say that prices increased by 3.6 percent during the 12-month period. You can do the same for any other years. If the CPI in January 1997 was 159.4, and if it were 162.8 in May 1998, then prices increased 162.8/159.4 = 1.021 times over the 15 month period.

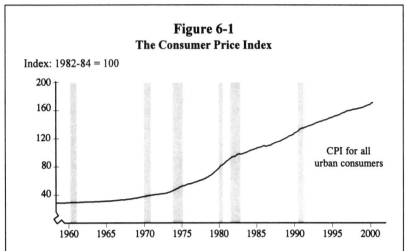

Figure 6-1
The Consumer Price Index

The consumer price index tells us little other than how the level of prices in one period compares to another. To find the rate of inflation, we have to compute, and then annualize, monthly or quarterly changes in the CPI.

The Politics of the CPI

Because of the enormous political and economic impact of the CPI, it is constantly under scrutiny. One of the more memorable was in 1996 when a special Congressional commission reported that the measure overestimated the annual cost of living by nearly 1.1 percent.[3] At the time, the main culprit was the fixed market basket which had not been updated since 1982-1984. The problem, now largely fixed, was that the market basket did not account for the substitution effects that occur when consumers use one product rather than another, nor did it take into account changes in shopping patterns that occur when consumers shop at discount outlets. Finally, quality improvements to existing products such as VCRs and computers tend to get overlooked.

The commission also reported that a 1-percentage point annual reduction in the CPI would reduce the federal deficit by about $1 trillion over 12 years—savings due to lower cost-of-living payments to social security recipients, higher receipts from taxpayers as tax bracket adjustments become smaller, and lower costs of other federal

---

[3] The Congressional Advisory Commission on the CPI was headed by Michael J. Boskin, a former Chairman of President Bush's Council of Economic Advisors.

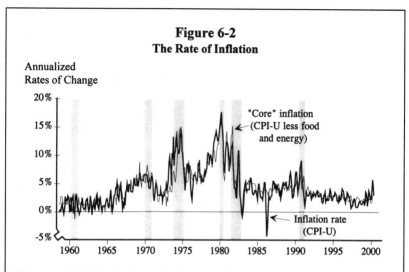

Figure 6-2
The Rate of Inflation

The rate of inflation is determined by annualizing monthly or quarterly changes in the CPI. The so-called "core" rate of inflation is only slightly more stable than the overall rate.

programs that are indexed by the CPI. This, of course, added a political element to the revision as the Federal government was struggling to balance its budget at the time.

The BLS did address some methodological issues raised by the commission, and the CPI numbers are better for it. Even so, the CPI today is neither more nor less than it ever was: a measure of the average change over time in the prices paid by urban consumers for a market basket of consumer goods and services.

The Consumer Price Index in Brief

Indicator status:	None
Compiled by:	Bureau of Labor Statistics
Frequency:	Monthly
Release date:	8th through 19th of the following month
Revisions:	Seasonal revisions in January for up to 5 years
Published data:	*Economic Indicators*, Council of Economic Advisors
	CPI Summary News Release, Bureau of Labor Statistics
Internet:	http://stats.bls.gov/cpihome.htm
	http://www.EconSources.com
Hotline update:	(202)691-6994

The Producer Price Index

Another important price series is the ***producer price index (PPI)***, which measures average changes in selling prices received by domestic producers for their output. Until 1978 the series was known as the *wholesale price index*, but the title was changed to emphasize that the series measures only price changes between the producer and the *first* purchaser of the product. It does not measure price changes that occur between other intermediaries such as the final wholesaler and the retailer who buys the product for resale to the public.

Coverage and Reporting

Every month, over 100,000 price quotations are obtained from virtually every sector of the U.S. economy, including both goods and service industries. Price indices are then prepared for three major groups—finished goods, intermediate goods, and crude goods—with final reports made available for more than 10,000 individual products and product groups. The index series in the PPI are reported with 1982 = 100 as the base year.

The Historical Record

Figure 6-3 shows the level of the PPI for finished goods in comparison to the CPI (or CPI-U to be exact). The figure shows that there is a fairly close relationship between the two measures, although for several reasons the PPI has fallen behind in recent years. For one thing, the PPI measures price changes only when the product is sold by the original producer. If several intermediaries are involved after this sale takes place, the profit margins taken by each will drive up the final retail price. For another, the PPI does not cover imported items, as does the CPI.

Historically, most of the interest in producer prices has focused on their eventual impact on consumer prices. If prices go up at the factory, the reasoning goes, then consumers will pay more later on.

Figure 6-3
Producer Prices and the Consumer Price Index

Index: 1982 = 100

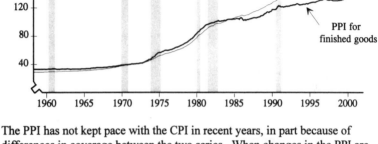

The PPI has not kept pace with the CPI in recent years, in part because of differences in coverage between the two series. When changes in the PPI are plotted over 3- or 6-month spans, the series appears much like Figure 6-2, with prices rising late in the expansion and then slowing or declining shortly thereafter.

Increases in the PPI can lead to increases in the CPI, but for the reasons given above, the linkage is not as close as it once was. Percentage changes in the PPI for 1-month and 3-month spans can also be computed, but like the CPI, none of the series have leading, lagging, or coincident indicator status.

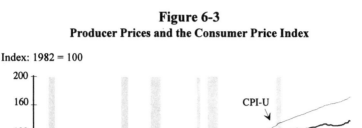

The Producer Price Index in Brief

Indicator status:	None
Compiled by:	Bureau of Labor Statistics
Frequency:	Monthly
Release date:	Second week of the following month
Revisions:	Up to 4 months after the initial monthly release
Published data:	*PPI News Release*, Bureau of Labor Statistics
	Economic Indicators, Council of Economic Advisors
Internet:	http://stats.bls.gov/ppihome.htm
	http://www.EconSources.com
Hotline update:	(202)691-5200 for the PPI

The Money Supply

Economists think of money as anything that serves as a unit of account, a medium of exchange, and a store of value. However, the exact definition of money is complicated by the fact that it takes so many different forms, ranging from coins to Eurodollar deposits.[4]

Definitions of Money

The Fed employs several definitions of money, two of which correspond to the functions of money described above.[5] One is called *M1* and is the transactional component of the money supply, or the part most closely identified with money's role as a medium of exchange. As can be seen in Table 6-2, this definition of the money supply includes coins, paper currency, traveler's checks, demand deposits, NOW accounts, credit union share drafts, and other checkable deposits.

If we want to consider money's role as a store of value as well as a medium of exchange, the definition is expanded to include other, and sometimes lesser known, forms of holding money. These include overnight retail repurchase agreements, savings deposits (including money market deposit accounts), balances in retail money market mutual fund accounts, and small denomination time deposits. This broader-based definition of money is known as *M2*. The individual components of M1 and M2 are presented in Table 6-2.

The Historical Record

Since the money supply is managed by the Federal Reserve System, we would expect that some variations in the money stock are possible over time. Figure 6-4 shows the levels of M1 and M2 from

---

[4] Dollar-denominated bank deposits in foreign countries, not necessarily in Europe.

[5] A total of four definitions—M1, M2, M3, and DEBT—are used by the Fed. See the *Federal Reserve Bulletin* for more on measures of M3 and DEBT.

Table 6-2

Components of the Money Supply, Billions of Current Dollars

1.	Coins and paper currency	$517.9
2.	Traveler's checks	8.2
3.	Demand deposits	341.3
4.	Other checkable deposits (NOW accounts, share drafts)	248.0
	M1	**$1,115.4**
5.	Savings deposits	
	(includes money market deposit accounts)	1,774.4
6.	Small denomination time deposits	
	(includes retail repurchase agreements)	981.2
7.	Retail money market funds	888.3
	M2 = (M1 plus lines 5-7)	**$4,759.3**

Source: *Statistical Release H.6*, May 11, 2000, Federal Reserve Board of Governors

1958 to the present. According to the figure, both definitions of money tend to rises steadily over time, but without regard to changes in economic activity.

So Why is M2 a Leading Economic Indicator?

It turns out that money, like any other commodity, can also be measured in terms of current or constant dollar amounts, the latter being preferable if we want to compensate for the distortions of inflation. If the two series shown in Figure 6-4 are converted to constant dollar amounts, they would both well function as leading indicators for recessions and recoveries. In fact, M2 has historically been included in the ***index of leading economic indicators*** that is now compiled by The Conference Board.[6]

The process of converting M1 or M2 to constant dollar measures is not difficult, but it is not done by the Fed—which is the reason that only current dollar amounts are shown here. Instead, the Fed only reports its money statistics in current terms, leaving the conversion to The Conference Board for its leading indicator index.[7]

---

[6] The list of component series that make up the *index of leading indicators* is on page 34.

[7] To make the conversion, monthly M1 and M2 figures are divided by the implicit price deflator for personal consumption expenditures, and then multiplied by 100. This is a legitimate conversion, but not one done by the source agency, and therefore not one designed to make M1 or M2 in constant dollars an everyday economic statistic.

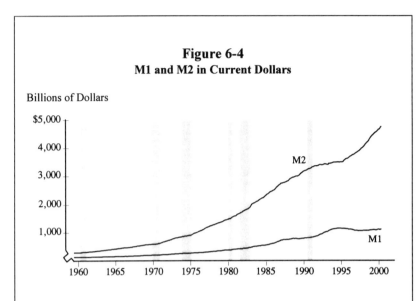

Figure 6-4
M1 and M2 in Current Dollars

Billions of Dollars

The levels of M1 and M2 have leading indicator status only when converted to constant dollar amounts, a transformation not performed by the Federal Reserve System.

Finally, some studies have found a strong, if somewhat delayed, link between changes in the level of M2 and prices. Because of this, many economists like to keep an eye on changes in M2 since it may indicate changes in the rate of inflation later on.

M1 and M2 in Brief

Indicator status:	Both series: leading for recessions, recoveries, and overall
Compiled by:	Federal Reserve Board of Governors
Frequency:	Weekly
Release date:	4:30 p.m. Thursdays for the previous week
Revisions:	None
Published data:	*Statistical Release H.6,* Fed Board of Governors
	Federal Reserve Bulletin, Fed Board of Governors
Internet:	http://www.federalreserve.gov
	http://www.EconSources.com
Hotline update:	None

The Fed Funds Rate

Fed funds, or *federal funds,* are excess reserve balances that banks and other financial institutions lend to one another on a short-term basis. The interest paid to borrow these funds is known as the *fed funds rate*. Most loans are overnight, although some may be for as long as three days.

Fed Funds

Historically, member banks of the Federal Reserve System were required to keep deposits at the Fed as reserves against savings accounts and checking deposits. Since the Fed did not pay interest on these reserves, member banks had little incentive to keep more funds than they needed. However, if a bank had excess reserves, it would often lend the surplus to another member bank on an overnight or weekend basis for a small fee. Banks that borrowed the excess reserves often did so to shore up their own reserves at the Fed.

When the loans were made, the funds never really left the Fed—hence the term "federal" in the title. All a member bank needed to do to make a transaction was to notify the district Fed bank that reserve funds were to be transferred from its account to another bank's account for a short period of time, after which the funds would be transferred back. Today the market for federal funds is far more sophisticated and is dominated by brokers who facilitate transfers.[8]

Over time, federal funds took on a more generic meaning as the practice of borrowing one another's reserves expanded to financial institutions outside the Federal Reserve System.[9] Today, financial institutions tend to deal with one another through the Fed since all depository institutions have access.

---

[8] The daily effective fed funds rate is a weighted average of rates on trades through N.Y. brokers. Rates are annualized using a 360-day year.

[9] Nonmember state banks, for example, might lend reserves to one another under this system.

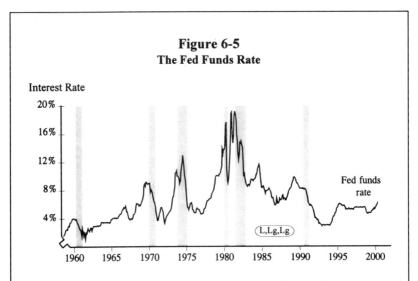

Figure 6-5
The Fed Funds Rate

Fed funds are short-term reserves that banks and other financial institutions lend to each other overnight, or for a few days at a time. The fed funds rate is the only interest rate that acts as a leading indicator for recessions.

A Leading Indicator

The history of the federal funds rate since 1958 is presented in Figure 6-5. Like all other interest rates in the economy, it has an overall classification as a lagging indicator.

Unlike other interest rates, however, it is the *only* interest rate that behaves as a leading indicator for peaks in overall economic activity.[10] As such, it is usually the first interest rate in the economy to turn down in the face of an impending recession.

This behavior is in part due to the way the Federal Reserve System conducts monetary policy. If the economy shows signs of slowing or even entering a recession, the Fed may pump excess reserves into the banking system to add liquidity. This stimulates the

---

10 The discount rate on new 91-day Treasury bills and the yield on long-term Treasury bonds are both coincident indicators for peaks in economic activity. The yields on high-grade corporate bonds and secondary market yields on FHA mortgages, as well as the average prime rate charged by banks, are all lagging indicators when it comes to predicting peaks in economic activity.

economy by lowering the price that other banks pay for borrowed reserves. The Fed is also likely to keep the rate relatively low until the recovery is well underway, so the Fed Funds rate does not begin to turn up until well after the recession has ended—making the series a lagging indicator for recoveries.

Because the federal funds rate is the only interest rate classified as a leading indicator for peaks in economic activity, it can serve both as an indicator for future changes in real GDP and as a leading indicator for movements in other interest rates.

The Fed Funds Rate in Brief

Indicator status:	Leading for recessions, lagging otherwise
Compiled by:	Federal Reserve Board of Governors
Frequency:	Daily
Release date:	Daily
Revisions:	None
Published data:	*Federal Reserve Bulletin*, Fed Board of Governors
	Statistical Release H.15, Fed Board of Governors
Internet:	http://www.federalreserve.gov
	http://www.EconSources.com
Hotline update:	None

The Discount Rate

In its role as a central bank and "lender of last resort," the Federal Reserve System is required to lend funds to other financial institutions. The *discount rate* is the interest rate the Fed charges on these borrowed funds. The term "discount rate" is, however, a misnomer since virtually all loans made by the Fed are in the form of advances rather than discounts.

Most important, the discount rate is not a competitive rate—it is a policy tool used to control the money supply. As such, the discount rate is an administered rate that affects the general level of credit, and eventually employment, prices, and overall economic activity.

Early Development

When the Fed was first established in 1913, the discount rate was intended to be the primary tool of monetary policy. Soon, however, the Fed discovered that interest rates could also be affected by buying and selling government bonds, a function now managed by the Federal Open Market Committee (FOMC).

It may seem redundant to have an independently determined discount rate coexist with FOMC activities, but this arrangement has two advantages for the Fed. First, the discount rate is set in conjunction with the regional Fed banks, fostering the appearance of participation in the monetary policy decision-making process.[11]

---

[11] An article in *Economic Commentary* by the Federal Reserve Bank of Cleveland explains how the discount rate is set:

> The mechanics of setting the discount rate are not complicated. The Board of Directors of each of the 12 Federal Reserve Banks is required to recommend a rate setting for its Bank to the Board of Governors of the Federal Reserve System no less frequently than every two weeks. If the Board of Governors approves the recommendation, typically it will notify any of the other 12 Banks that have not made the same recommendation so that their Boards of Directors have an opportunity to act simultaneously. If the Board of Governors thinks that a change is called for when none of the 12 Banks has recommended a change, it may make informal efforts to elicit a recommendation (July 15, 1989.)

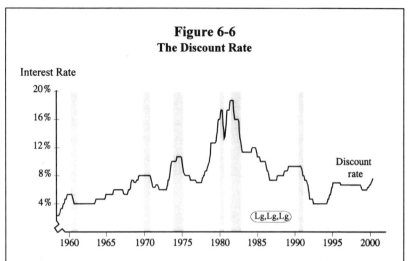

Figure 6-6
The Discount Rate

The discount rate is the interest rate that borrowers pay when obtaining a loan from the Fed. It is a tool of monetary policy and therefore has no formal status as an indicator of future economic activity.

Second, it generates an "announcement effect" which serves as a source of policy information for Fed watchers.

The Historical Record

Because the discount rate is discretionary, it changes only infrequently. The rise of the discount rate at the end of each expansion reflects the Fed's concern with controlling inflation as much as anything. It has no official status as an economic indicator, even though it appears to lag changes in overall economic activity.

The Discount Rate in Brief	
Indicator status:	None
Compiled by:	Federal Reserve Board of Governors
Frequency:	Daily
Release date:	Daily
Revisions:	None
Published data:	*Federal Reserve Bulletin*, Fed Board of Governors
	Statistical Release H.15, Fed Board of Governors
Internet:	http://www.federalreserve.gov
	http://www.EconSources.com
Hotline update:	None

The Treasury Bill Rate

The *Treasury bill rate* is one of the most important short-term interest rates in the economy. Treasury bills (T-bills) are available to a wide range of investors, and they are auctioned weekly and traded daily.[12] As a result, the rate on T-bills reflects the most current market forces of supply and demand.

The Historical Record

The history of interest rate movements for T-bills appears in Figure 6-7. For purposes of comparison, the prime rate is also shown.

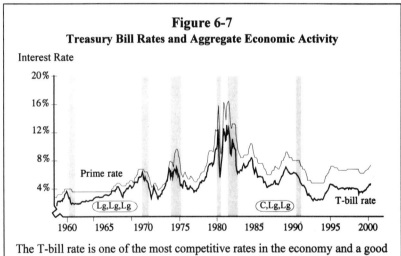

Figure 6-7
Treasury Bill Rates and Aggregate Economic Activity

The T-bill rate is one of the most competitive rates in the economy and a good indicator of changes in the supply and demand for funds. In comparison, the predominant prime rate tends to adjust to the T-bill rate after a brief lag.

---

[12] A Treasury bill is a short-term obligation with a maturity of 13, 26, or 52 weeks. T-bills have minimum denominations of $10,000 and do not pay interest directly because they are sold on a discount basis. For example, an investor may purchase a 52-week bill for $9,300. The $700 difference between the amount paid and the amount received at maturity is the investor's interest. The $700 return on the $9,300 investment is a yield of $700/$9,300 = 0.0753, or 7.53 percent.

Since the T-bill rate adjusts so quickly to market forces, it changes earlier than the prime rate. The series behaves as a coincident indicator for peaks in the economy, meaning that the rate turns down when the economy turns down.

It also behaves as a lagging indicator when the economy recovers from a recession, meaning that the economy recovers before the T-bill rate recovers. The overall classification of the series, like that of *all* other interest rate series, is that of a lagging indicator.

Treasury bills are traded continuously during market hours, and so rates are available daily. Summary information is published by the Fed and most financial newspapers. Because the T-bill rate is so competitive, many adjustable-rate financial securities, including some home mortgages, are tied to them.

The Treasury Bill Rate in Brief

Indicator status:	Coincident for recessions, lagging otherwise
Compiled by:	Federal Reserve Board of Governors
Frequency:	Daily
Release date:	Daily
Revisions:	None
Published data:	Most financial newspapers
	Economic Indicators, Council of Economic Advisors
	Federal Reserve Bulletin, Fed Board of Governors
	Statistical Release H.15, Fed Board of Governors
Internet:	http://www.federalreserve.gov
	http://www.EconSources.com
Hotline update:	None

The Prime Rate

Historically, the *prime rate* was the rate banks charged their best customers. Because of this, it received wide publicity as the lowest rate available from banks. Things have changed some since then, and so the prime rate today is not quite the same as it used to be. Despite these changes, it is still widely watched.

If You Get the Prime Rate, Do You Actually Pay It?

That depends. Suppose a business borrows $100,000 at a 10 percent prime rate. However, the company may not get to use all the funds because the bank may require a *compensating balance*, or a deposit (usually interest free), in the amount of $5,000. On a simple interest basis, the company is really paying $10,000 to get the use of $95,000, for a 10.53 percent simple rate.

Another bank may have an identical prime but a different compensating balance requirement in the amount of $10,000 per $100,000 borrowed. A borrower at this bank would still pay 10 percent on the $100,000 for an interest cost of $10,000 but have access to only $90,000, for an 11.11 percent simple rate.

The Historical Record

The Fed determines the predominant prime rate by surveying the 25 largest banks in the country, shown in Table 6-3, as ranked by total asset size. Once the predominant prime is established, the Fed waits for the majority of the banks to adopt a new rate before the prime is recomputed.

Figure 6-8 shows that the prime rate appears to adjust in steps, or stages. That is, it stays at one level for a while before it adjusts to a new one. There are two reasons for this. First, banks are more inclined to change the compensating balance requirement than the prime, especially when interest rates are rising. Second, the official

Table 6-3

Banks Used to Determine the Predominant Prime Rate

Boston	Fleet National Bank
	State Street Bank and Trust Company
New York	Bank of New York
	Bankers Trust Company
	Chase Manhattan Bank
	Citibank, N.A.
	HSBC Bank, USA
	Morgan Guaranty Trust Company
	Summit Bank
Cleveland	FirstStar Bank
	Keybank N.A.
	Mellon Bank, N.A.
	National City Bank
	PNC Bank, N.A.
Richmond	Bank of America N.A.
	First Union National Bank
	Wachovia Bank of N.C., N.A.
Atlanta	AM South Bank
	Southtrust Bank N.A.
	Regions Bank
Chicago	Bank One N.A.
St. Louis	Union Planters Bank N.A.
Minneapolis	U.S. Bank, NA
San Francisco	Wells Fargo Bank, N.A.
	Union Bank of CA, N.A.

Source: The Federal Reserve System, Division of Monetary Affairs, May 16, 2000.

prime rate statistics compiled by the Fed represent the prevailing level rather than an average of the existing rates charged by banks.

Because banks can increase effective interest rates by changing the compensating balance, the prime is a lagging indicator for both recessions and recoveries. Changes in the prime rate usually make headlines, but the changes normally reflect other interest rate

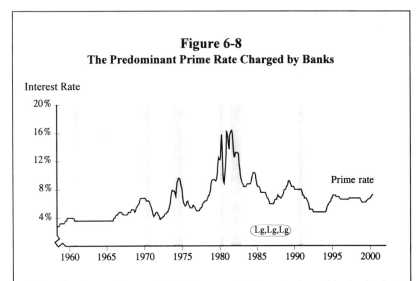

Figure 6-8
The Predominant Prime Rate Charged by Banks

This series is sometimes called the "average" prime rate charged by banks, but it's clearly *not* the average. If 13 banks in the Fed sample charge a prime rate of 7 percent, and if the remaining 12 charge 9 percent, the predominant prime will be 7 percent.

adjustments that have already taken place. Occasionally, a prominent bank not on the list may change its rate, and the action may be widely reported in the press, but it will have no effect on the official predominant prime rate statistics compiled by the Fed.

The Prime Rate in Brief

Indicator status:	Lagging for recessions, recoveries, and overall
Compiled by:	Federal Reserve Board of Governors
Frequency:	Daily
Release date:	Daily
Revisions:	None
Published data:	*Federal Reserve Bulletin*, Fed Board of Governors
	Statistical Release H.15, Fed Board of Governors
Internet:	http://www.federalreserve.gov
	http://www.EconSources.com
Hotline update:	none

Chapter 7

FINANCIAL MARKETS, INTERNATIONAL TRADE, AND FOREIGN EXCHANGE

The Dow Jones Industrial Average

The *Dow Jones Industrial Average* (*DJIA*) is one of the oldest and most widely-quoted measures of stock market performance in the world. It is used as a proxy for the price movements of stocks issued by more than 3,000 companies that are listed on the New York Stock Exchange (NYSE).

The DJIA includes 30 representative firms, and the size of the index depends on the market price of each firm's stock at any given time. If the prices of the stocks in the average are rising, the DJIA goes up and the market is also presumed to be going up. If the prices of the 30 stocks are falling, the DJIA goes down, indicating that other stocks in the market are also presumed to be going down. Over time, some firms are deleted and others added, but the total number of stocks is kept at 30.

Early History

In 1884 the Dow Jones Corporation began to publish the average closing price of 11 active stocks in its *Customer's Afternoon Letter*, a short publication that later evolved into *The Wall Street Journal*. By 1886 the average included 12 stocks, and by 1916 it was expanded to 20. Finally, in 1928 it was expanded to include 30 stocks. These stocks, listed in Table 7-1, have changed occasionally over the

Table 7-1

The 30 Stocks in the Dow Jones Industrial Average

AT&T	Exxon	McDonald's
American Express	General Electric	Merck & Co.
Alcoa	General Motors	Microsoft
Boeing	Hewlett-Packard	Minnesota Mining & Mfg.
Caterpillar	Home Depot	Morgan, J.P.
Citigroup Inc.	Honeywell	Phillip Morris
Coca Cola	IBM	Procter & Gamble
Disney	Intel	SBC Communications
DuPont	International Paper	United Technologies
Eastman Kodak	Johnson & Johnson	Wal-Mart Stores

Source: *Bloomberg Online*, May 16, 2000.

years to keep abreast of changes in the economy. Figure 7-1 explains one of the more popular charts used to present short-term movements of the average.

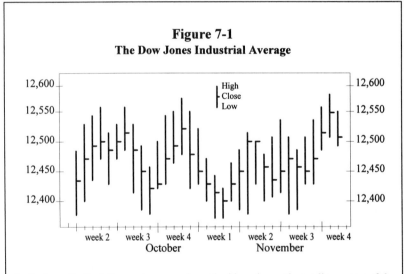

Figure 7-1

The Dow Jones Industrial Average

In the hypothetical figure above, each vertical bar shows the trading range of the DJIA during the course of a single day, with the nub on the side of the bar representing the closing value. Note that we cannot tell when the high and low values were reached; the chart tells us only the range.

But, Is It *Really* an Average?

In 1884 the index really was an average, but it proved difficult to maintain because of the problem caused by stock splits. For example, consider a simple DJIA which, on Monday, had three stocks priced $20, $30, and $40. The DJIA for that day would be ($20 + $30 + $40)/3 = $30, or simply 30. Next, suppose that nothing happens on Tuesday except for a two-for-one split of the $20 stock (instead of holding one share of a stock worth $20, you now own two shares worth $10, and so your wealth remains unchanged).

If we computed the DJIA on Tuesday by dividing the prices of three shares ($10, $30, and $40) by 3, the DJIA would drop to 26.7, even though investors would be no worse off than before. We could, however, compensate for the drop in the average by adjusting the *divisor*. Instead of dividing the sum of the prices by 3, we could divide by 2.667 so that the "average" would be ($10 + $30 + $40)/2.667 = 30, just as before.

Whenever a stock splits or whenever stocks on the list are replaced, the divisor can be adjusted to keep the overall average from being affected. Of course, this means that the divisor must be revised frequently. By 1939, for example, the divisor was about 15; by 1950 it was below 9, and by 1981 it had reached 1.3. On May 12, 2000, the divisor was 0.18238596, which means that the DJIA computation was as follows:

$$DJIA = \frac{\text{sum of 30 prices}}{\text{divisor}} = \frac{\$1,935.00}{0.18238596} = 10,609.37$$

We can now definitely say that the Dow Jones Industrial Average really *is* an average . . . in a manner of speaking.

Are 30 Stocks Enough?

Despite the small number of stocks included in the DJIA, the companies are so large that the DJIA represents about 25 percent of the total value of all stocks on the New York Stock Exchange. As a result, the movement of the DJIA coincides fairly well with that of a large number of stocks on the exchange.[1]

---

[1] For comparison purposes, a chart of the DJIA appears with the S&P 500 in Figure 7-2.

The 30 companies in the DJIA do not represent the smaller companies on the exchange, nor do they normally represent other firms listed on the American Stock Exchange, or even any of the other regional exchanges around the country. In fact, until October 1999, all of the companies in the DJIA were listed exclusively on the NYSE. The exception occurred when Intel and Microsoft, companies listed on the Over-The-Counter market, were added in an attempt to give a bigger role to technology stocks.

Why Update the DJIA?

The main reason for updating the companies in the DJIA is to make the sample more reflective of the changing conditions in the economy. For example, in April 1991, the composition of the index was changed to better reflect the size of the services sector. Navistar, Primerica, and USX were dropped from the index, while Caterpillar, Disney, and J.P. Morgan were added.

By the late 1990s, the NASDAQ, the stock index that tracks the progress of stocks listed on the Over-The-Counter Market, was beginning to perform better than the DJIA—beating it three out of four years in a row. As a result, Intel and Microsoft took the place of Chevron and Goodyear even though they were listed on a different exchange. At the same time, Union Carbide and Sears were dropped in place of SBC Communications and Home Depot. This means that 7 of the 30 firms in the sample were replaced in less than a decade.

When firms are replaced in the DJIA, no historical revisions or other changes are made other than to adjust the divisor. All that is done is to select a new divisor so that the DJIA remains unchanged during the transition. So, if a low-priced stock is replaced by a higher one, the divisor is increased on the following day.

Are There Other Things We Should Know?

There are probably two worth mentioning. First, any price-weighted average like the DJIA gives more weight to higher-priced stocks than it does to lower-priced ones. For example, a 10 percent increase in the price of J.P. Morgan (trading near $132 in May 2000) adds $13.20 to the numerator of the equation above. A 10 percent increase in the price of Philip Morris (trading near $28 at the same time) adds only $2.80 to the numerator.

The other weakness of the DJIA is that it does not adjust for stock dividends of less than 10 percent.[2] This means that it understates long-term gains in the market. Stock prices will not tend to rise as fast if some companies declare relatively small and relatively frequent stock dividends.

Because the series is updated so frequently and because of the visibility given to it by the Dow Jones Corporation which publishes *The Wall Street Journal*, it is a useful measure of short-term movements of stock prices on (predominately) the New York Stock Exchange. When stock price movements over longer periods are of concern, researchers usually turn to other series that have a broader sample and are not biased by stock dividend payouts.

Finally, the Dow Jones Industrial Average is regarded by many as a leading indicator of future economic activity, with the index turning down before a recession begins and then turning up before the economy turns up. It is not the series of stock prices used by The Conference Board for its *index of leading indicators* (Standard & Poor's 500 is used instead), but as you can see in Figure 7-2, the two series are fairly close.

The Dow Jones Industrial Average in Brief

Indicator status:	Leading indicator for peaks and troughs
Compiled by:	Dow Jones & Co.
Frequency:	Continuously during market hours
Revisions:	None
Published data:	*The Wall Street Journal* and in the stock market section of most newspapers
	Economic Indicators, Council of Economic Advisors
Internet:	http://dowjones.com
	http://www.EconSources.com
Hotline update:	none

---

[2] Theoretically, a stock dividend (a dividend paid in stock, rather than cash) *lowers* the company's stock price. If a firm in the 30-company sample declares an 8 percent stock dividend, the number of shares outstanding goes up by 8 percent and the price goes down by a like amount—leaving investors with no change in net wealth. However, the divisor for the DJIA remains unchanged, so the DJIA would actually show a decline.

Standard & Poor's 500

Another popular measure of stock price performance is *Standard & Poor's 500* (S&P 500) composite index. Standard and Poor's Corporation published its first market index of 233 stocks in 1923. By 1957 the list had expanded to a total of 500 stocks. Today, those 500 stocks represent four major industry groupings: industrials, public utilities, transports, and finance.[3]

How Are the Firms in the Index Selected?

One criteria is based on industry groupings. The market is first divided into approximately 100 subgroups ranging from aerospace to toys. Then, representative companies are selected for each industry grouping. In some cases, the firms in the subgroups are relatively small, with modest stock issues outstanding. A second criteria is that the shares of a company are liquid enough to be fairly priced. Companies that are closely held, or do not otherwise have a competitive market for their shares, are excluded from the index.

Finally, and unlike the DJIA, the companies in the sub groupings are not primarily listed on the NYSE; many are listed on the American Stock Exchange and the Over-The-Counter market. While the companies in the S&P 500 do not necessarily include the largest ones on the New York Stock Exchange, approximately 80 percent of the total value of the NYSE stocks are represented in the index.

How Is the Index Computed?

The S&P 500 is not a price-weighted average like the DJIA; it is a *value-weighted index* reflecting the total market value of a company's stock. For each company in the sample, the total number

---

[3] Until 1988, the 500 stocks consisted of 400 industrials, 40 utilities, 20 transportation companies, and 40 financial institutions. When a company in one category was dropped, it was replaced by another company from the same category. The number of companies in each category now varies somewhat over time.

of shares of the company's stock is multiplied by the individual price per share to get the total market value of that stock.[4] The market value for each of the remaining 499 stocks is computed in the same way, and the results are added together to get the current market value of all 500 stocks in the index. The resulting total would be huge, of course, but when indexed to a base period (1941-1943 is currently used), the numbers become more manageable.

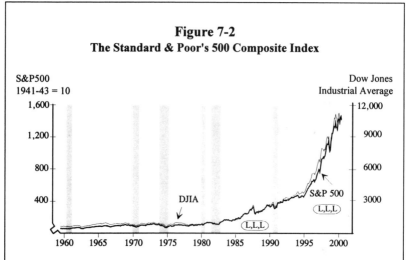

Figure 7-2
The Standard & Poor's 500 Composite Index

The S&P 500 is a value-weighted index, while the DJIA is a price-weighted index. Despite this difference and the difference in sample size, the two series behave in a similar manner over time.

The series, shown in Figure 7-2, is different from most other indices in that it has a base value of 10 rather than 100. So, if the index closes at 1450, the total market value of all stocks in the S&P 500 is 145 times higher (1450/10) than it was in the 1941-1943 period.

Is the S&P 500 Better Than the DJIA?

Different perhaps, but not necessarily better. It is more representative since 500 stocks are covered rather than 30. In

---

[4] A company with 3 million shares of common stock outstanding, valued at $15 a share, would have a total market value of (3,000,000)($15) = $45,000,000.

addition, the value-weighted nature of the index means that it automatically adjusts for splits and stock dividends.[5] As can be seen in Figure 7-2, the S&P 500 and the DJIA are fairly close despite the difference in the sample size used by each.

In addition to its role as a proxy for stock price movements, the index generally works so well as a leading indicator of future economic activity that it is used in The Conference Board's composite *index of leading indicators*.

Standard & Poor's 500 in Brief

Indicator status:	Leading for recessions, recoveries, and overall
Compiled by:	Standard & Poor's Corporation
Frequency:	Almost continuously
Release date:	Daily
Revisions:	None
Published data:	Stock report listing in most daily papers
	Economic Indicators, Council of Economic Advisors
Internet:	http://www.standardandpoors.com
	http://www.EconSources.com
Hotline update:	none

---

[5] Suppose that a company listed in the S&P 500 declares a 5 percent stock dividend. The number of shares would go up by 5 percent and the price of the shares would go down by a corresponding amount, leaving the total market value of the stock—and the level of the S&P 500—unchanged. If that same company happened to be one of the 30 DJIA stocks, the index would fall slightly because the price of one of the stocks in the numerator would fall, *without* any compensating change in the divisor.

The Trade Deficit

When a country engages in international trade, several formal sets of accounts are used to track the flow of international transactions. The best-known, is the **balance on goods and services** which replaced the *balance on merchandise trade* account in 1994.[6] The word "balance" in the title allows for the possibility of a surplus as well as a deficit. However, because imports have exceeded exports for so long, our trade statistics are commonly—although improperly—called the *deficit on goods and services* accounts.

NIPA (Again)

Trade statistics, like many other statistics generated by the U.S. Department of Commerce, are directly related to the national income and product accounts. Table 7-2 (a version of Table 2-3 on page 24) follows the familiar approach of dividing the economy into sectors. This time we want to focus on the foreign sector, otherwise known as "net exports of goods and services," to see how the *balance on goods and services* is computed.

The advance figures in current dollars for the first quarter of 2000 show the total value of all exports at $1,043.7 billion. This was offset by imports of $1,378.7 billion, leaving a $335 billion deficit in the balance on goods and services. These numbers are reported on an annualized basis and show the net balance that would occur if exports and imports remained unchanged at the current rate for the entire year. The export and import categories are further divided into goods (merchandise) and services, with the table showing goods exports of $734.4 billion and imports of $1,165.8 billion—from which we can calculate a $431.4 billion deficit.[7]

---

[6] At the time, the services component of the trade balance was running a substantial surplus, so the overall impact of combining goods with services was to sharply reduce the trade deficit.

[7] This is the *balance on merchandise trade* which has been in deficit continuously since the first quarter of 1976.

Table 7-2

NIPA and the Goods and Services Trade Balance, Billions of Dollars

	Current	Constant (1996$)	%GDP
Gross domestic product	*$9,697.2*	*$9,156.6*	*100.0*
Personal consumption expenditures	*6,615.2*	*6,225.2*	*68.2*
Gross private domestic investment	*1,709.9*	*1,724.2*	*17.6*
Net exports of goods and services	*-335.0*	*-377.1*	*-3.5*
Exports	*1,043.7*	*1,077.7*	*10.8*
Goods	734.4	783.1	7.6
Services	309.3	295.6	3.2
Imports	*1,378.7*	*1,454.8*	*14.2*
Goods	1,165.8	1,246.4	12.0
Services	213.3	210.3	2.2
Government consumption & gross investment	*1,707.1*	*1,565.2*	*17.6*

Source: *Survey of Current Business.* First quarter 2000 advance estimates; some totals may not
add due to rounding.

Collecting and Reporting the Data

In practice, data for exports and imports of goods are collected
continuously by the Bureau of the Census from declarations filed with
the U.S. Customs Office by international shippers. Other techniques
are used to estimate the monthly volume of services. Because of the
nature of the data, trade figures are normally released 45 days after the
close of the reference month.

The Census Bureau releases trade figures in several formats.
Initial trade figures are reported monthly, and year-to-date figures are
obtained by adding up the trade balances for individual months.[8]
Annualized figures, such as those shown in Table 7-2 and Figure 7-3,
are estimated by the BEA and published as part of the NIPA. This
means that the size of the trade deficit will be small if the report is for
the month, approximately 3 times larger if the report is for the quarter,
and approximately 12 times larger if the numbers are annualized.
Accordingly, we have to be careful not to confuse a relatively large
monthly figure with a relatively small quarterly one.

---

[8] The June 20, 2000 *International Accounts Data Trade in Goods and Services* report from
the Bureau of Economic Analysis listed goods and services balance at $-27.4 billion for
January, $-28.1 for February, $-30.6 for March and $-30.4 for April—for a year-to-date
deficit of $116.6 billion.

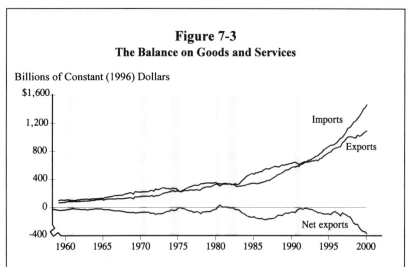

Figure 7-3
The Balance on Goods and Services

The United States has had a persistent goods (merchandise trade) deficit since the first quarter of 1976. The balance on goods and services, shown as the difference between the two series at the top, or plotted separately in the lower part of the figure, provides a more comprehensive measure of the trade picture.

In Figure 7-3, annualized quarterly data are used to show the balance on goods and services from 1958 to the present. The balance can either be shown as the difference between goods and services exports and imports (shown at the top of the graph) or it can be plotted separately, as shown at the bottom of the figure.

Finally, we still don't have the whole international picture unless we take a look at the *balance on current account* which requires two further adjustments to the net exports of goods and services. First, we have to add income generated from U.S. assets held abroad, and then subtract any payments made because of foreign assets in the U.S. Second, we have to take into account net unilateral transfers made abroad: government grants to other nations; pension and social security payments to people living in other countries; and, payments made by private individuals to family members, political organizations, and religious movements in other countries.

Despite the more comprehensive measure provided by the current account balance, the trade balance on goods and services is perhaps our primary international trade statistic, or at least the one that gets the most attention. This balance, in turn, is affected by (1) our demand for foreign-made products and (2) our ability to sell domestically produced goods abroad. The trade figures on goods and services are important because they affect employment in the export and import industries as well as the value of the U.S. dollar.[9] Because dollars are paid to foreigners to make up for the deficit, larger deficits generally mean that more dollars go abroad, and more dollars circulating relative to other currencies make the dollar worth less.

Goods and Services Trade in Brief

Indicator status:	None
Compiled by:	Bureau of the Census
Frequency:	Monthly, quarterly
Release date:	45 days after close of reporting month
Revisions:	One month back for seasonally adjusted data, 6 months back for constant dollar series, annual revisions in June
Published data:	*Report FT900*, Bureau of the Census
	Economic Indicators, Council of Economic Advisors
Internet:	http://www.census.gov/foreign-trade/www
	http://www.EconSources.com
Hotline update:	(202)606-5306 for GDP statistics and its components

---

9 The relationship between the value of the dollar and the trade deficit is fairly straightforward. A strong dollar, as was the case in the mid-1980s, usually causes imports to rise faster than exports, which causes the trade balance to worsen. Eventually, the additional dollars that go abroad cause the international value of the dollar to fall, which reverses the trend in exports and imports and improves the trade balance.

International Value of the Dollar

When we talk about the value of the dollar, we are referring to its purchasing power in terms of other currencies. However, we can't evaluate the strength of the dollar by following just one or two exchange rates. Instead, we have to see how the dollar performs against a broader group or bundle of currencies. Historically the primary measure was called the *exchange*, or *trade-weighted value of the U.S. dollar,* and it was prepared by the Federal Reserve System.

Over time, however, world trade patterns changed and currency evolutions such as the emergence of the European Union's euro took place. As a result, the Fed retired the old series and replaced it with a broader one called the *broad currency index*. This new series has two components, one of which overlaps the old series.

Out With the Old . . .

The original series was created when the world went to flexible exchange rates in 1971. At the time, the Fed decided to compile an index using a group of 10, or G-10, major industrialized countries that were substantially involved in world trade.[10]   The weight of each country's currency was based on the amount of global trade each one had relative to the other countries in 1971, the year flexible exchange rates were adopted. After the relative weights were determined, the series was given a base of 100 for March 1973.

During this period, the G-10 series, illustrated in Figure 7-4, served as the main measure of the dollar's strength.[11] The series went up when the dollar got stronger, and went down when the dollar got weaker relative to the other 10 currencies.

---

[10] The ten countries in the sample—Belgium, Canada, France, Germany, Italy, Japan, Netherlands, Sweden, Switzerland and the United Kingdom—were also chosen because they participated in the Smithsonian Accord of December 1971.

[11] The term "G-10" did not seem to come into use until after the Fed introduced the new broad currency index. As a result, the term "exchange" or "trade-weighted value of the dollar" is still applied to the new series by some parts of the Fed.

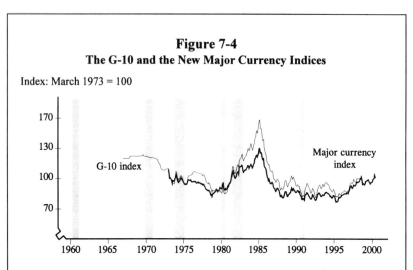

Figure 7-4
The G-10 and the New Major Currency Indices

Index: March 1973 = 100

The *G-10 Index*, formerly known as the *exchange value of the U.S. dollar*, was our most comprehensive measure of the dollar's international strength until it was discontinued in 1998. The *major currency index* that takes its place is a subset of the new *broad currency index*.

Eventually the 1971 fixed base weights became outdated, and the introduction of the euro affected five of the ten currencies in the index. As a result, the G-10 series was discontinued in 1998.

... And In With the New

The more comprehensive replacement series is simply called the ***broad currency index***, and is made up of currencies from 35 countries. Unlike the G-10 index, the weights are not fixed, but are adjusted over time as trade patterns change. This index is computed in both nominal and real (inflation adjusted) terms, but the latter is the one most important for historical comparisons.

On a nominal basis, the broad index starts with a value of 32 in 1973, and then it increases steadily until it reached 120 in mid-2000. While this may seem odd, the broad index contained a number of high-inflation countries that experienced severe currency depreciations. When the series is converted to real terms, as in Figure 7-5, the basic trend of the U.S. dollar's value is more apparent.

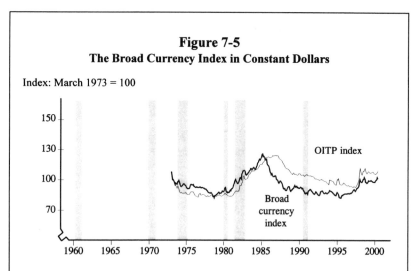

Figure 7-5
The Broad Currency Index in Constant Dollars

Index: March 1973 = 100

The *Broad Currency Index* is now the most comprehensive measure of the International value of the dollar. The series includes both the *major currency index* and the *Other Important Trading Partner (OITP)* index.

A subset of the broad index is the *major currency index*. This index has 16 countries and is more comparable to the G-10 index, which is why the two are shown together in Figure 7-4. Even though the weighting and sample sizes are different, it is clear that the two series behave about the same.

The last series is the *OITP Index*, which is short for "other important trading partners." This index consists of 19 countries that are in the broad index, but excludes those in the major currency index.[12] Many of the currencies of these countries are not traded extensively outside their home markets, although they are important U.S. trading partners. Because many of these countries also experienced high inflation and occasional currency problems, the OITP index is computed in price-adjusted, or real terms, whenever long periods of time are involved. For shorter periods, any of the series in nominal terms are adequate.

---

[12] The OITP includes currencies from Argentina, Brazil, Chile, China, Columbia, Hong Kong, Israel, India, Indonesia, Korea, Malaysia, Mexico, Russia, Saudi Arabia, Singapore, Taiwan, Thailand, The Philippines, and, Venezuela.

So Why Are These Series Important?

The large changes in the international value of the dollar shown in Figures 7-4 and 7-5 have an enormous impact on the nation's exports and imports—and hence employment in those industries. When the purchasing power of the dollar is high, as in the mid-1980s, a large number of products are imported, leading to employment growth in those industries that utilize these imports. At the same time, however, American products are much more expensive abroad, leading to layoffs in the export industries. These forces are reversed when the value of the dollar falls, as it did in the early 1990s, causing a feast or famine situation for everyone as the dollar goes from strength to weakness, and then eventually back to strength again.

Changes in the value of the dollar also affect the balance of trade. When the purchasing power of the dollar is high, imports are relatively inexpensive and our exports relatively costly to foreign buyers, which eventually results in a worsening balance of trade. When the value of the dollar falls, the situation tends to reverse itself, resulting in an improved balance of trade.

Value of the U.S. Dollar in Brief	
Indicator status:	None
Compiled by:	Federal Reserve Board of Governors
Frequency:	*H.10* weekly, *G.5* monthly
Release date:	*H.10* Monday for the previous week ending Friday, *G.5* last day of month for the reporting month
Revisions:	None
Published data:	*Federal Reserve Bulletin,* Fed Board of Governors *Statistical Release G.5*, for monthly rates *Statistical Release H.10*, for daily rates
Internet:	http://www.federalreserve.gov http://www.EconSources.com
Hotline update:	None

Foreign Exchange

When we talk about foreign exchange in the context of international trade or finance, we are usually referring to the number of other currency units that can be purchased with one U.S. dollar. The amount of a single foreign currency that can be purchased with the dollar is called the *foreign exchange rate*, and there are well over 200 exchange rates in the world today.

Currency Units per Dollar and Dollar Equivalents

One popular way to express an exchange rate is in *American terms*, or in the number of U.S. dollars needed to buy a single foreign currency unit. For example, if one euro costs $0.9192, then 0.9192 is the U.S. dollar equivalent of one euro. Likewise, if the cost of a single yen is $0.009216, the U.S. dollar equivalent of one yen is 0.009216.

Table 7-3
Foreign Exchange Rates

	U.S. $ Equivalents (American terms)	Foreign Currency Units per U.S. $ (European terms)
Britain (Pound)	1.5169	0.65926084
EMU Members (Euro)	0.9192	1.08790
Germany (D-Mark)	0.4700	2.1278
Japan (Yen)	0.009216	108.51
South Korea (Won)	0.0008983	1113.25

Source: *Wall Street Journal,* data are for May 12, 2000.

The second way to express an exchange rate is in *European terms*, or in the number of foreign currency units that are equal to one U.S. dollar. The two terms are simply reciprocals and are shown in Table 7-3 above. For example, if one euro costs $0.9192, then one dollar is worth 1.0879 euros (1.0879 is the reciprocal of 0.9192).

Likewise, one dollar would be equal to 108.51 yen (the reciprocal of 0.009216).

Currency Cross Rates

If we want to know the exchange rate between two currencies, we could express everything in terms of cross rates, as in Table 7-4. This is especially helpful when neither of the currencies being traded is the U.S. dollar.

Table 7-4
Currency Cross Rates

	U.S. $	Won	Yen	D-mark	Euro	Pound
Britain	0.6593	0.00059	0.00608	0.3099	0.6060	–.–
EMU Mbrs.	1.0879	0.00098	0.010025	0.51128	–.–	1.6502
Germany	2.1278	0.00191	0.0196	–.–	1.9559	3.227
Japan	108.51	0.09747	–.–	50.9963	99.7426	164.4737
S. Korea	1113.25	–.–	10.2594	523.1930	1023.30	1688.5333
U.S.	–.–	0.0008983	0.00922	0.02273	0.9192	1.5169

Source: Computed from Table 7-3 (reciprocals may not match due to rounding)

In the table, the value of each currency unit is expressed in terms of other currencies. For example, if one U.S. dollar buys 2.1278 D-marks, and if one U.S. dollar buys 1,113.25 Korean won, then one DM is worth 1,113.25/2.1278 = 523.1930 Korean won. Likewise, if a dollar can purchase 108.51 yen, and if a dollar can purchase 1.0879 euros, then one euro is worth 99.6500 Japanese yen.

Foreign Exchange Rates in Brief

Indicator status:	None
Compiled by:	Federal Reserve Board of Governors
Frequency:	*Statistical Releases G.5* monthly *H.10* weekly, daily
Release date:	*H.10* Monday for the previous week ending Friday, *G.5* last day of month for the reporting month
Revisions:	None
Published data:	*The Wall Street Journal* for previous the day *Statistical Release H.10*, for daily NYC noon buying rates
Internet:	http://www.federalreserve.gov http://www.EconSources.com
Hotline update:	None

Appendix

Chain Weighting

Chain-weighted calculations are hardly intuitive, so they are probably best explained with an example such as the one below which has only two product groups: computers and everything else. Before we begin, we should note that the examples are loosely modeled after Table 2-1 on page 17 of the text. You may want to review that table first before proceeding.

In the first year of our abbreviated economy, 2 units (Q) of computers are sold at an average price (P) of $10. Five units of everything else are sold at $10, generating a first-year GDP of $70. Similar calculations for the next year show a new GDP of $99, a 41.43 percent gain over the first. In tabular form, the data would look like this:

Table 1
GDP Growth in Current Dollars:

Year 1	Q	P	(P)(Q)	Year 2	Q	P	(P)(Q)
Computers:	2	$10	$20	Computers:	4	$6	$24
Everything Else:	5	10	50	Everything Else:	5	15	75
			GDP = $70				GDP = $99

One-year growth in GDP = $99/$70 = 1.4143, or 41.43%

And yet, a closer look at Year 2 reveals that the robust 41.43 percent growth was due almost entirely to inflation in the "everything else" category. In fact, because computer prices went down so much, consumers only spent $4 more on computers in year 2 than they did in the previous year.

If we try to compensate for inflation by using base-year prices that are fixed in the first year, as in Table 2, we can see that the estimated growth for GDP is quite different, and much lower:

Table 2
GDP Growth Using Constant (Year 1) Prices:

Year 1				Year 2			
	Q	P	(P)(Q)		Q	P	(P)(Q)
Computers:	2	$10	$20	Computers:	4	$10	$40
Everything Else:	5	10	50	Everything Else:	5	10	50
		GDP =	$70			GDP =	$90

One-year growth in GDP = $90/$70 = 1.2857, or 28.57%

Or, we could compute GDP growth using constant year 2 prices as in Table 3, which gives us an even *lower* growth estimate:

Table 3
GDP Growth Using Constant (Year 2) Prices:

Year 1				Year 2			
	Q	P	(P)(Q)		Q	P	(P)(Q)
Computers:	2	$6	$12	Computers:	4	$6	$24
Everything Else:	5	15	75	Everything Else:	5	15	75
		GDP =	$87			GDP =	$99

One-year growth in GDP = $99/$87 = 1.1379, or 13.79%

If we want to adjust for inflation by using a set of fixed or base year prices, which of the two methods is theoretically superior: estimates using first year prices, or estimates using second year prices? Both have advantages and disadvantages, but it is clear that there is a "weighting effect"—a distortion that takes place because those quantities which have increased the most are usually associated with goods, such as computers, whose prices have declined the most relative to other prices.

The solution to the problem of the optimal base year is to find the geometric mean of the two index numbers. This is done by computed the square root of their product. In other words, the computations would appear as:

$$\sqrt{(1.2857)(1.1379)} = 1.2095, \text{ or } 20.95\%$$

This geometric average is also called the "Fisher Ideal" index number, and is the basis for BEA's chain-weighted prices that are now used in place of the fixed base-year weighted prices employed until 1995.

Despite the theoretical superiority of the geometric mean, BEA's changeover at the beginning of 1996 was not without controversy. For example, second quarter growth in 1995, formerly reported at +.5 percent, was revised downward by .7 percent to -.2 percent. Likewise, the revisions also meant that the growth of real GDP during recent expansions was actually .5 percent less than previously reported.

Index